COUNTRY KITCHEN

FRANCES BISSELL is one of Britain's most highly regarded food writers. She is the author of a number of books, including *Modern Classics*, with her husband Tom, *An A–Z of Food and Wine in Plain English* and, most recently, *Entertaining*, all published by Macmillan.

Also in the Pan Cooks series

Darina Allen – Simply Delicious Suppers

Annie Bell – Evergreen

Simon Hopkinson – Gammon & Spinach

Claudia Roden – Invitation to Mediterranean Cooking

Jeremy Round – The Independent Cook

Frances Bissell

Country Kitchen

PAN BOOKS

First published 1996 by Macmillan

This edition published 2002 by Pan Books
an imprint of Pan Macmillan Ltd
20 New Wharf Road, London N1 9RR
Basingstoke and Oxford
Associated companies throughout the world
www.panmacmillan.com

ISBN 0 330 39168 2

9 8 7 6 5 4 3 2 1

A CIPcatalogue record for this book is available from the British Library.

Typeset by SX Composing DTP, Rayleigh, Essex
Printed and bound in Great Britain by
Mackays of Chatham plc, Chatham, Kent

This book is dedicated to all

the kind and charming people

I met in the West Country

and to the memory of

Mr Gordon Collins

Contents

Introduction

Living and cooking in a converted Cornish water-mill

As a cook and cookery writer working in England, how can I not be influenced by the rich cornucopia that is the West Country? We spend a good deal of time in Britain complaining about the weather, but it is our geographical situation and our variable island climate that we have to thank for the abundance and variety of produce we are able to enjoy year round. True, we do not have long growing seasons, but for me part of the pleasure of cooking is to be able to make the most of particular foodstuffs during their short season. I do not mind waiting until June for strawberries, and I look forward to the first mainland crops of tomatoes from Cornwall. Thanks to the high rainfall, we have lush pastures in Devon and Cornwall. These enable our dairy herds to produce rich milk, which in turn is made into clotted cream, butter, and fine farmhouse cheeses which are becoming the envy of the world. Native breeds of cattle, the ruby North Devons and the brighter South Devons, graze as they have done for centuries, growing slowly, feeding naturally and allowed to gain their finished weight at the right time, unhurried by hormones and growth promoters. Sheep graze the higher ground, producing marvellous spring lamb.

Not all is tradition. Enterprising farmers are rearing sheep for milk used in some of the best cheeses in the country. Goats are being reared for meat, and thriving in the healthy Dorset countryside. On the other hand, some ancient traditions are being revived. Not only do the fine orchards of Somerset produce superb eating apples and excellent cider, but distilled apple spirit is being made once again. Richly flavoured fruit liqueurs are made in Devon after the summer harvest of soft fruit. Some West Country vineyards are producing wines of an exceedingly good quality, especially when we have good summers. I have tasted outstanding red wine from the 1990 vintage, and look forward to the 1995 being ready to drink. Old water-mills have been restored and are once again milling wheat into stone-ground floor as they have done since medieval times. And rare English breeds of pigs are being reared in preference to modern slim-line crosses. These animals, too, are reared to high standards and produce, as you would expect, fine pork, bacon and ham.

I was thrilled to be asked by Westcountry Television to write and present a cookery series for them, and it was not difficult to reach the conclusion that a substantial part of each programme should focus on the people who produce all the good things the West Country has to offer. To me it was a great delight to seek out these dedicated farmers, growers and producers, to learn how and why they work as they do, and then to use the products of their labours in my kitchen. Often I was reminded of the time I spent in the West Country as a child, on family holidays. Clotted cream was probably the first 'exotic' food I ever tasted.

I wrote much of this book in Cornwall, and when I first came here in the early part of 1995 to begin work on my television series, I could not help but be struck by Cornwall's 'otherness' and the feeling that I was in another country, increasingly so as I travelled west.

Home was a converted water-mill on the hillside overlooking the village of Lanlivery with its pub, the excellent Crown, and its church of St Brevita. At the outset, the director, Peter Francis Browne, and I agreed that a studio kitchen would not be appropriate, and he set out to look for somewhere not only for me and my husband Tom to live, but somewhere with a big enough kitchen for filming. The Mill at Threthew, owned by Sheila and Gordon Collins, was the first place he saw, and my husband Tom and I knew just from photographs that we could live there quite happily. Just down the road from the Mill was Lostwithiel, one of the ancient Cornish stannary towns, where tin was assayed, or checked, for purity. A corner or 'coin' of tin was cut from each block for testing.

One evening over a cold and windy Easter, when we had a few days off from filming, I read about this part of Cornwall in one of the excellent Shell Guides. This is what it told me:

> Lanlivery stands on a bare shoulder of land, swept by the south winds and overlooked by the brooding mass of Helman Tor, a granite outcrop 687 ft above sea level. Between the tor and the slate-roofed farmhouses that crowd around the village church lies a squelchy heathland known as Red Moor, as ancient as the rock itself and with a hint of mystery.
>
> Unfenced lanes wander nearby, passing tin workings not used since pre-Christian times and crowded over with

willow, broom and gorse. Looming above the scene on the tor is a huge rocking stone, a precariously balanced boulder that sways in the wind.

For 500 years from medieval times, prospectors went 'steaming' for tin on Red Moor, sieving it from running streams, rather in the way that gold miners 'pan' for gold. Lanlivery is now a dairy-farming centre, fanning out around the pub and the church, which has a turreted tower reaching 97 ft into the sky. One side of the tower used to be painted white, to stand out as a landmark for sailors off Gribben Head, 6 miles to the south-east.

No satisfactory explanation has ever been found for the name Lanlivery. 'Lan' or 'nant' in Cornish means 'churchyard'. The rest is obscure, although it is believed that 'livery' may have been a personal name. Even the dedication of the church is uncertain. It is named St Brevita, or Bryvyth, but parishioners believe that the true patron saint is St Dunstan, the 10th-century reforming Archbishop of Canterbury. Lanlivery holds its feast day in the month of St Dunstan's Day (May 19th). The existing church dates from the 15th century, when an earlier building was restored, and has a font large enough for total immersion.

Outside the church entrance is a large, lidless stone coffin. There is no inscription, but the coffin is said to have once contained the body of a Cornish prince, carried from the chapel at Restormel Castle, a few miles to the north-east on the banks of the River Fowey, when the chapel was secularized.

A board on the church tower dated 1811 carries a bell-ringer's rhyme, recording that anyone who mars a peal shall 'pay sixpence for each single crime to make him cautious against another time.'

This, then, was our home for a good part of 1995. In fact we lived continuously at the Mill for longer than at our flat in London. Any doubts I had about townies transplanting to the country were gone in a very short time.

For shopping, nearby Lostwithiel and Fowey supplied much of what we needed. And because I was there to learn more about local produce, we travelled far to seek out butchers, fish-mongers and cheesemakers. Where possible, we eschewed those modern cathedrals to convenience, erected on the outskirts of old Cornish towns, St Asda, St Tesco, St Somerfield with Gateway, although their car parks, I must admit, produced useful rendezvous points on our journeys up the A38 and down the A30.

Fish has never been so good or so fresh as what I bought in the West Country. At Fowey Fish, they sell the catch landed from a small boat which puts into Looe. One day it might be small John Dory and red mullet with which I would make a fish stew. Another day, a large, stiff, shiny brill, which I had filleted: I then simply floured the fillets, fried them in olive oil and served them with mashed potatoes and parsley sauce. I gave similar treatment to John Dory that I had bought with John Strike of the Quayside Fish Centre in Porthleven, when he took me to the morning fish auction at Newlyn. Both beam trawlers and day boats had unloaded, the first with huge mono-catches of megrim and haddock, the second with smaller catches of a wide variety of fish.

Occasionally, as a treat, if we did not have to be on the road too early for that day's shoot, I would cook the Mill breakfast; good sausages and bacon were put into a dish, and baked in the top oven of the Aga, the sausages going in first, if they were thick. Then I drained off the fat, and cracked in a few free-range eggs, and then put the dish back in the oven for a few minutes, until the eggs were set. The eggs were truly free-range, sometimes from our neighbour's bantams. To begin with, the hens and geese were quite neighbourly, but they soon realized what I got up to in my kitchen and went to great lengths to avoid us. The pheasants did not. They flaunted themselves, knowing that October was still a long way off.

When we first arrived, the primroses were hardly to be seen. Then, after Easter, they carpeted the Cornish hedges, interspersed with bluebells, campions and wild garlic. The hawthorn hedges changed from being thorny, black spindles to soft drifts of green. Nettles grew thickly by the mill pond, and a soup of nettles as a starter for the evening's dinner, perhaps with some wild garlic, if I could find a patch in the untamed part of the garden, was on my mind more than once. But I never got round to it.

Returning to Cornwall in high summer was a delight and a revelation after living there in the somewhat bleak spring. It was hard to imagine that there could be so many shades of green, each unique and intense, from the pale green of newly mown meadows to the dense, flat green of sycamores and the glossy bright, dappled green of ivy around tree trunks. Flowers in the hedgerows were no longer the whites and yellows of early spring but rather the dusty blues, pinks and bright reds of high summer, with wild fuchsias dripping their purple and scarlet blooms everywhere.

The mill pond was patrolled by large iridescent dragonflies, like helicopters from nearby St Mawgan. Nestling thrushes had grown up into greedy, ungainly adolescents. I caught two of them pestering their mother early one morning, gobbling worms as fast as she could find them. But it was a family under stress; the day before, when I had been sitting writing at the kitchen table, I heard a sharp crack and thud against the full-length window. As I turned, all I saw were two or three soft, small feathers fluttering to the ground. I looked out and saw a handsome, bright male thrush on its back, legs just stiffening, as it died of a broken neck. And, while I know *we* missed the hedgehog late one night a mile from Lostwithiel, I am not sure it escaped the driver behind us. As we reached the Mill and turned into the drive, we disturbed a barn owl which batted its wings slowly across the garden like a soft, giant moth. It then disturbed our sleep through the night, as we had disturbed it.

The muscat vine which covers the inside of the conservatory already had bunches of large grapes in June. And the leaves, large but not yet leathery, were at the perfect stage for stuffed vine leaves. In that sun and heat, the herbs were thriving, and as you brushed past them, the garden smelled of Provence.

Here it was easy to think of the perfect summer meal: paper-thin slices of Denhay ham with peaches or melon, or smoked Cornish mackerel with a cucumber relish to start. Earlier in the year, I was cooking slow roasts and braised pork. Now I only wanted to cook fish, which was in superb condition everywhere. When we ate at Piermasters in Plymouth's Barbican, Steven Williams suggested we have line-caught sea bass, which had just been delivered that evening. These were big fish that were filleted, grilled and served bathed in Tuscan olive oil. Not far away, local cod was on the menu at Chez Nous, where Jacques Marchal cooked me a thick neck piece with a pesto crust – a fine, simple dish.

Lloyd Downes at Plymouth's Pannier Market is the chefs' favourite local fishmonger, and it was from him I bought a beautiful River Tamar salmon, a lovely sleek, silver fish: some to eat at the Mill, some to cure like gravadlax, but with mixed herbs from the garden instead of dill, and take back to London. To go with the salmon: Cornish whites, really nice potatoes, and some locally grown broad beans. Somerset Brie, Cornish Yarg, Ticklemore Goat and Devon Blue will follow. Pudding will be the simplest, most seasonal imaginable – a heap of English strawberries, a bowl of clotted cream, and another bowl of light muscovado sugar. Not a hint of black pepper; not a smidgen of sherry vinegar; not a dash of balsamico; just plain English strawberries and cream. And what strawberries! All shapes and sizes, and a sweet intensity of flavour that I have not experienced for a long time.

On our way down the winding track to the Mill, as we arrived from London, I picked a bundle of elderflowers, probably the last of the season, and made cordial, which kept us and our visitors going through the hot weather, well diluted with chilled, sparkling mineral water. And having discovered Plymouth gin, gin and tonic was an occasional pleasure. I have never been very keen on gin and tonic, but I have now devised a version much more to my taste. The usual gin, or the 100-proof version, if you can get it, a thin sliver of lemon peel, just a little tonic water, and plenty of sparkling mineral water. It's much less sweet this way. On the other hand, for a superb cocktail, with a real flavour of English summer, add a dash of elderflower cordial to your gin and tonic.

When Tom and I returned to the Mill in winter to film the Christmas series, hot spiced cider and mulled wine were the things we wanted to drink. They were what I prepared for the carol singers who came one evening from St Brevita's, to go with the mince pies, almond shapes and hazelnut macaroons.

One evening we were enjoying a quiet dinner by the fire when we heard a tap at the door. On opening it, we found three men in flat caps and warm jackets standing each on a different step, ringing a peal of bells with silver handbells. It was a beautiful, haunting crystal-clear sound on the night air.

But most of the time it was bustle, dealing with plump turkeys, joints of pork and medieval Christmas pies, not to mention all the trimmings and desserts. The kitchen was the centre of the activity, the Aga working at full throttle, day and night, as I sometimes cooked our lunchtime soups overnight. Lovely garlands of scented pine, holly and other evergreens hung from the mantel above the Aga, and a bunch of greenery was stuck in a plain and simple glazed salt jar. After we'd finished the last day of cookery filming, I couldn't stop cooking, so stayed up most of the night making mincemeat for the film crew with all the leftover dried fruits, nuts and brandy.

In this book you will find far more than the recipes which I cooked in the television series. I have included the recipes I have developed over the years as a result both of my travels in the West Country and of the inspiration I draw from its wonderful produce.

Vegetables

Whilst we do not have in this country the farmers' markets and wholefood supermarkets which one finds all over North America, we do have some very good farm shops and dedicated individuals who are keen that we should be able to eat organic food if we want it. Some of the most enterprising are those who get the vegetables right to your door, through vegetable box schemes. Guy Watson of Caddaford Farm, as well as supplying his brother Ben's Riverford Farm Shop in Buckfastleigh, Devon, operates a weekly delivery of vegetable boxes to drop-off points in the area. He also produces a useful booklet describing the more unusual vegetables and salad stuffs, with excellent recipes and a wealth of tips, well written, authoritative and uncondescending. Guy Watson is as concerned about how we cook his produce as he is about growing it, following sustainable agricultural and horticultural practices. You don't have to peel his carrots. The day we went to film, the barn at Caddaford Farm, where they pack the vegetable boxes, was stacked with vivid, healthy-looking roots, fruits and greens, particularly the brassicas, including kale, purple sprouting broccoli, mizuna (see page 30) and rocket.

Thoby Young describes his London-based Fresh Food Company as a 'virtual farmers' market', recognizing that the way in which markets are licensed and operate in Britain does not favour growers taking their produce to market, as in the American farmers' market system. Suppliers of vegetable boxes work with farmers, both locally and nationwide, to develop sustainable agricultural systems that do not require the use of pesticides. Soft fruit, for example, is grown with the help of aphid-eating ladybirds, instead of harmful sprays. The Fresh Food Company's weekly, fortnightly or monthly vegetable box scheme, though London-based, operates nationwide, with subscribers from Cornwall to Scotland.

In both cases, and in other vegetable box schemes, of which there are a number throughout the country, whilst the prices remain constant, the content and weight of the box will vary with the seasons, being at their richest in summer and autumn. Just imagine the pleasure of unpacking a box of fresh organic vegetables next week: there might, depending on the season, be new potatoes with skins so fine you can rub them off in your fingers, perfect with asparagus and a free-range egg to dip them in; satiny globe artichokes to eat with vinaigrette, sweet crisp cucumbers for a dill-flavoured salad, peppery rocket in a generous bunch, enough for you to stir into a bowl of pasta, and fresh peas and broad beans. Or you might unpack sweet nutty root vegetables, parsnips, celeriac, carrots and swedes, perfect for roasting round the Sunday joint, and a big enough bunch of parsley to make into soup.

Herbs have always been important in English cookery. Gervase Markham, writing in 1615 in *The English Housewife*, said that the first step to skill in cookery was 'to have knowledge of all sorts of herbs belonging into the kitchen; whether they be for the Pot, for Sallets, for Sauces, for servings or for any other seasoning or adornment'. Many of the herbs that we use now were introduced to England for cultivation long before 1615. Tarragon vinegar and pesto might seem modern developments, but Dorothy Hartley in *Food in England* (1954) reports that in Ireland in the 1900s, during the potato famine, she came across a preparation which she referred to as 'pesto', using basil, marjoram, parsley, onion or garlic, salt, pepper and 'a bit of old dry cheese', pounded together, mixed to a paste with boiling water, enriched with bacon fat or dripping, and poured over a hot cereal base and raw greens. Florence White in *Good English Food* (1952) comments that tarragon vinegar was 'commonly used in England for flavouring dishes over a hundred years ago'. In using herbs in our cooking, we are simply following our native culinary heritage.

Most often herbs are used in savoury dishes, but they do have a place in puddings and desserts. David Wilson, of the Peat Inn in Fife, combined rosemary with chocolate, and created a unique chocolate mousse. Caroline Liddell and Robin Weir in their excellent book *Ices* have developed the idea and produced a chocolate and rosemary ice cream. Experiment with infusing the herb in chocolate to make simple chocolate sauce. Leaves of bay, lime, sweet geranium, cicely and thyme can be used to flavour custards. Chef Willi Elsener at the Dorchester uses basil seeds in an ice-cream. I sometimes poach pears in red or white wine with a leaf or two of sage or a sprig of rosemary. And, of course, I use fresh mint in fruit pies and crumbles.

A quick guide to the best methods of cooking vegetables

Steaming and stir-frying: broccoli, beans, bean-sprouts, cabbage, cauliflower, chard, Chinese greens, courgettes, kohl rabi, peas, spinach, spring greens

Boiling: artichokes, cardoons, potatoes, salsify

Braising: cabbage, celery, chicory, fennel, leeks, okra

Baking: celeriac and other roots, onions

Roasting/grilling: aubergines, peppers, courgettes, tomatoes, mushrooms and all root vegetables

Purées: all root vegetables and tubers, pumpkins and other winter squashes, plantain

Parsley and Potato Soup | serves 4

This is a very easy soup recipe, the basis of many vegetable soups, which you can adapt to whatever herbs and vegetables you have available. In the summer, I make a chilled basil and potato soup.

2 potatoes, peeled and chopped
1 onion, peeled and chopped
1 tablespoon sunflower oil
115g (4oz) parsley
about 1.25 litres (2 pints) vegetable or light chicken stock
handful of fresh herbs, such as parsley, chives, chervil and sorrel
sea salt and freshly ground black pepper
3–4 tablespoons plain yoghurt or single cream (optional)

Fry the potato and onion gently in the oil for a few minutes without browning.

Rinse, drain and roughly chop the parsley and add most of it to the pot. Add about 150 ml (¼ pint) stock, and cook until the vegetables are soft. Add half the herbs and cook for a few minutes more.

Allow to cool slightly, add the rest of the herbs and parsley and make a purée in a blender or food processor. Sieve, and stir in the rest of the stock. Reheat, season to taste, and stir in the yoghurt or single cream if using. This soup is also very good chilled.

Celeriac, Saffron and Cheese Soup | serves 4–6

Pale root vegetables are much enhanced by the colour and deep, complex flavour of saffron. Saffron potatoes, either mashed or simply boiled, have become something of a cliché, but they nevertheless taste very good, as does this inexpensive soup using celeriac, which is at its best in the winter, tender and sweet, rather than woody and bland.

good pinch of saffron strands
1 medium onion, peeled and sliced
25g (1oz) butter, or 2 tablespoons sunflower oil
1 head of celeriac
1 heaped tablespoon plain flour
about 1.25 litres (2 pints) vegetable or chicken stock
2–3 tablespoons single or double cream
3–4 heaped tablespoons grated hard cheese, such as Cheddar
sea salt and freshly ground black pepper

Let the saffron soak in a little hot water while you gently fry the onion in the butter or oil until soft. Peel the celeriac and dice or slice. Add it to the onion, cook it in the butter or oil in the pot for a few minutes, then sprinkle on the flour and stir, adding just a little stock. When this is well blended, gradually stir in the rest of the stock, and add the saffron liquid.

Cook until the celeriac is soft, blend and sieve the soup,

bring back to the boil, stir in the cream and cheese, then season to taste with salt and pepper.

Note

Michel Roux, at Le Gavroche, uses very thinly sliced scallops added at the last minute to a saffron and celeriac soup; well worth trying at home, in which case your stock could be a shellfish stock.

Summer Vegetable Soup | serves 8

Here is a recipe for when gardens, allotments and markets are positively bursting with produce.

55g (2oz) butter
500g (generous 1lb) shelled weight fresh garden peas
4 lettuce hearts, chopped
3–4 leeks, chopped
2 cucumbers, chopped
small bunch of fresh chervil, parsley and mint
2 litres (scant 4 pints) vegetable or chicken stock
sea salt and freshly ground black pepper
2 egg yolks
150ml (¼ pint) double cream

For the garnish
freshly cooked peas

Melt the butter in a large saucepan, and sweat the peas, lettuce, leeks and cucumber for about 10 minutes, without colouring. Add the herbs and the stock, and simmer until the vegetables are tender. The soup may be rubbed through a sieve or blended in a liquidizer, but this is not obligatory.

Season the soup with salt and pepper. Blend the egg yolks with the cream, and add to the soup. Heat through without boiling. Serve garnished with small cooked peas.

Carrot, Fennel and Apple Soup | serves 4–6

1 medium onion, peeled
6 carrots, peeled
1 medium fennel bulb, trimmed
1 medium Bramley apple, peeled and cored
1.25 litres (2 pints) vegetable or light chicken stock
2 bay leaves
sea salt and freshly ground black pepper

Dice or chop the vegetables and apple into roughly even-sized pieces. Put them into a saucepan with 300ml (½ pint) of the stock and the bay leaves. Cover with a lid, and cook very gently until the vegetables are tender.

Remove the bay leaves. Sieve or blend the vegetables with a little more stock until smooth, then return the mixture to the saucepan. Stir in the rest of the stock. Bring to the boil, then simmer for 5 minutes, season with salt and pepper and serve.

Tomato and Garlic Soup with Lovage | serves 6–8

Here is a lovely summer soup when everything in the garden is at its ripest and sweetest, and herbs in full leaf.

about 1kg (generous 2lb) ripe tomatoes
2–3 heads of new garlic
2 tablespoons sunflower, grapeseed or groundnut oil
1.25 litres (2 pints) vegetable stock
3–4 sprigs of lovage, or some celery tops
½ teaspoon freshly grated peeled ginger root, or a pinch of ground ginger
sea salt and freshly ground black pepper

Halve the tomatoes. Separate the garlic cloves, and peel them. Heat the oil in a heavy saucepan, and stir in the tomatoes and garlic. Cook until the juices begin to caramelize slightly, but without browning the vegetables. Add half the stock, the lovage or celery tops and the ginger, and cook until the garlic is soft. Allow to cool slightly, then blend and sieve, and return the liquid to the saucepan. Stir in the remaining stock, reheat, and season with salt and pepper before serving. This soup is also excellent chilled.

Herb and Almond Crisps | makes 18

Chilled vegetable soups are very good served with these crisp herb and almond biscuits.

1 free-range egg white
pinch of salt
55g (2oz) ground almonds
1 tablespoon finely chopped fresh herbs
½ teaspoon grated lemon zest
1 teaspoon cornflour
1 tablespoon finely grated hard dry cheese

Stir all the ingredients together, and spoon on to baking sheets lined with baking parchment. Bake in a preheated oven at 140°C/275°F/Gas 1–2 for 15–20 minutes until firm. Remove from the oven, and cool on a wire rack.

Herb Dumplings | serves 6

Although normally cooked in stews, dumplings can also be made in miniature versions and served in soup. Try these herb dumplings with a clear vegetable soup. Beef suet can be replaced by vegetarian suet, if appropriate. Dumplings can be made with a mixture of flour and breadcrumbs or breadcrumbs alone. The herbs used can, of course, be varied according to taste and availability, and more green colour obtained by the addition of cooked, dried and finely chopped spinach.

115g (4oz) fresh white breadcrumbs
115g (4oz) plain flour
1½ teaspoons baking powder
55g (2oz) finely chopped or grated suet
grated zest of 1 lemon
grated zest of 1 orange
1 spring onion, finely chopped
2 tablespoons fresh herbs, finely chopped
sea salt and freshly ground black pepper
2 free-range eggs, lightly beaten

Mix together all the dry ingredients, including the suet, citrus zest, spring onion, herbs and seasoning, and then bind to a soft dough with the eggs. With floured hands, form into small balls, or shape into quenelles with two wet teaspoons. Lower into boiling water or soup, and poach for 15 minutes or so.

Leeks Vinaigrette

Leeks are the main ingredient in this inexpensive, simple, quickly prepared dish that is a useful standby. It is also good enough to serve as a starter to a grand main course, particularly a rich one. It is a dish which can be dressed up with cubes of good saucisson or shredded ham. My father serves it with grilled or fried slices of black pudding, which is an excellent, if unusual, combination. Then you might add a poached or fried egg on top and serve it for lunch or supper.

4–6 thin leeks per person, fewer if you can only find the stouter ones
extra virgin olive oil
a squeeze of lemon juice or splash of cider vinegar
sea salt and freshly ground black pepper

Trim and clean the leeks carefully. Split them lengthways down towards the base without cutting right through. Rinse and drain. Drop them into boiling, lightly salted water, and cook until quite tender, 5–10 minutes depending on size. Alternatively, you can steam them.

Drain the leeks, and arrange them in a shallow dish. While still warm, sprinkle fairly liberally with good olive oil, a small squeeze of lemon juice or vinegar, salt and pepper. I would serve them while still slightly warm. Preparing them in advance and refrigerating them never seems quite as successful: the leeks begin to look dull, and their flavour is not improved.

Note

Seakale, asparagus and purple sprouting broccoli are also very good served like this.

Radish and Watercress Salad with Blue Cheese Dressing | serves 6–8

Packed in a box, with the dressing separate, this is a lovely dish to take on a picnic as, unlike many salads, it does not wilt too quickly. Or serve it for lunch in the garden.

1 cos lettuce
1 round soft-leaf lettuce
2 bunches of watercress
2 bunches of radishes

For the dressing
85g (3oz) West Country blue cheese, crumbled and at room temperature
2 tablespoons plain yoghurt or buttermilk
freshly ground black pepper

Trim, wash and dry the lettuces, and tear up the larger leaves, leaving the smaller inner ones whole. Heap in a salad bowl with clean, dry watercress sprigs. Wash and thinly slice the radishes, and add to the bowl.

To make the dressing, simply blend the cheese and yoghurt or buttermilk, thinning with a little milk or water, if you prefer a thinner mixture. Season with pepper, and pour the dressing over the salad just before serving.

Spinach, Rocket and Mizuna Salad | serves 4

Here is a dark green salad full of peppery, spicy flavour from the mizuna and rocket, two of the more unusual leaf vegetables Guy Watson grows in the spring. Mizuna, a member of the brassica family and widely grown in Japan, has glossy, dark green leaves, and when young and tender, makes a welcome addition to winter and spring salads.

4–6 rashers of smoked streaky bacon
4 good handfuls of leaves of spinach, rocket and mizuna
cider vinegar
walnut oil or extra virgin olive oil (optional)

Cut the bacon into matchsticks. Render it slowly in a frying pan, then cook more quickly to allow it to crisp.

Quickly wash the greens, and shake or towel them dry. Tear the spinach into manageable pieces. Place it with the rest of the leaves in a salad bowl. Pour on the hot bacon and its fat, and toss quickly. Sprinkle on a little cider vinegar, and serve immediately, adding oil if you think the salad needs it.

Salad of Peas, Fennel and Mint | serves 6

450g (1lb) shelled weight fresh green peas
1 large fennel bulb

For the vinaigrette dressing
2–4 sprigs of fresh mint
¼ teaspoon coarse sea salt
4 tablespoons walnut, hazelnut or olive oil
1 tablespoon cider vinegar
1 teaspoon clear honey
freshly ground black pepper

To make the vinaigrette dressing, strip off the mint leaves, and put them into a mortar with the salt. Grind to a paste, and gradually add the oil, vinegar and honey. Season with pepper.

Boil the peas for 2 minutes. Drain and refresh under cold running water. Put into a bowl with the dressing. Trim the fennel, and slice into thin segments. Add to the bowl, and stir gently so that all the ingredients are well coated before serving.

Note

When buying fennel, choose a nicely rounded bulb – the female, rather than the flatter male, which has far less flavour and not such a good texture. Scrubbed and boiled new potatoes also make a very good addition to the salad.

Asparagus Cream Tartlets | makes 12

225g (8oz) shortcrust pastry
350g (12oz) tender green asparagus
55g (2oz) crème fraiche or Greek yoghurt
sea salt and freshly ground black pepper
3–4 firm but ripe tomatoes

For the garnish
flat-leaf parsley

Roll out the pastry, cut into 12 rounds with a pastry cutter, and line 12 tartlet tins. Prick the pastry with a fork, and bake blind for 12–15 minutes in a preheated oven at 190°C/375°F/Gas 5.

Meanwhile, rinse the asparagus thoroughly, breaking the stems off where they become woody. Cut off the asparagus tips, and reserve these for garnish. Break the rest of the asparagus into pieces, and drop them into boiling salted water. Cook until completely tender. During the last minute or two of cooking time, steam the asparagus tips in a colander over the boiling water.

Drain all the asparagus. Put the tips to one side, and rub the rest of the stems through a sieve. Mix the purée with the crème fraiche or yoghurt, and season to taste with salt and pepper. Peel, seed and dice the tomatoes.

When the tartlet cases are cool, place a teaspoonful of

tomato in the bottom of each, pile the asparagus cream on top, and garnish with the asparagus tips and parsley.

Summer Vegetable Tart | serves 4–6

450g (1lb) mixed summer vegetables (such as carrots, broccoli, asparagus, courgettes, broad beans, peas, green beans)
225g (8oz) shortcrust pastry
3 free-range eggs
300ml (½ pint) full-cream milk
85g (3oz) grated hard cheese, such as Ticklemore Goat or Menallack
sea salt and freshly ground black pepper
freshly grated nutmeg

Prepare the vegetables as appropriate: peel and thinly slice carrots; break broccoli into florets; rinse asparagus, and break each stem into 3–4 tender pieces. Slice courgettes, shell broad beans and peas, and top, tail and slice or snap green beans or runner beans. Drop all the vegetables into boiling lightly salted water, and boil for 2 minutes only. Drain and refresh under cold running water. Broad beans are best if popped from their skins at this stage.

Roll out the pastry, and line a 25–30 cm (10–12in) flan tin or dish. Prick the base, line with greaseproof paper, fill with baking beans and bake blind in a preheated oven at 190°C/375°F/Gas5 for 8–10 minutes. Allow to cool slightly. Arrange the vegetables in the pastry case. Beat together the eggs, milk, grated cheese and seasonings, and pour over the vegetables. Extra cheese can be grated on top if you wish.

Bake in the oven at 200°C/400°F/Gas6 for about 25 minutes, until the filling is set, puffed up and golden. Serve cold, but not straight from the refrigerator.

Tomato Pudding | serves 10

Cornish tomatoes are the first of the mainland crop to come on to the market. Here is a recipe for high summer, when they are at their fullest and sweetest. It is made on the same principle as summer pudding, and makes a marvellously refreshing first course, appealing to meat-eaters and vegetarians alike. The original inspiration for this dish comes from that marvellous lady, Jennifer Paterson, who described it many years ago in her *Spectator* column. The pudding as I prepare it now is much removed from the Paterson original, so any shortcomings are mine, not hers.

about 1.5kg (generous 3lb) ripe tomatoes
sea salt and freshly ground black pepper
12–15 slices of firm white bread, crusts removed
extra virgin olive oil
sherry vinegar

For the garnish
sprigs of fresh herbs

Peel the tomatoes and cut them in half. Scoop out the seeds, juice and pulp and process all this with the skins. Chop the tomato flesh, and put it into a bowl. Rub the pulp and skins through a sieve to extract maximum juice and flavour. Pour half the resulting liquid on to the tomatoes. Taste the mixture, then add just enough salt and pepper to season. Season the remaining tomato liquid.

Cut the bread into wedges, dip into the tomato liquid, and line small moulds as if making individual summer puddings, or line a large pudding basin with the bread. Spoon in the chopped tomato, and cover with a round of bread. Cover the puddings, weight them, and refrigerate for 6–8 hours or overnight.

To serve, turn out on to a chilled plate, garnish with herbs, and serve with more tomato liquid mixed with olive oil and sherry vinegar. Accompany with steamed baby leeks, rocket salad or other greenery.

Celery and Smoked Salmon Parfait | serves 6

I'm not sure if this should be in the fish or vegetable chapter, but I think it should be here as it is the celery which adds the important flavour.

3 leaves of gelatine or 3 teaspoons powdered gelatine
1 head of celery
175g (6oz) smoked salmon, in one piece if possible
fresh chervil, lovage or flat-leaf parsley
115g (4oz) ricotta or cottage cheese
white pepper
150ml (¼ pint) whipping cream
2 free-range egg whites

Line a loaf tin with clingfilm. Soften the gelatine in a little cold water. Reserve the inner celery stalks to serve with cheese, and remove tough strings from the outer ribs. Chop these roughly, and simmer until tender in about 200ml (⅓ pint) water.

Dice half the smoked salmon into 5mm (¼in) cubes, and put to one side. Strain the celery cooking liquid into a bowl, and stir in the gelatine until dissolved. Take about 75g (3oz) of the cooked celery, and dice it small. Put the rest, when cool, in a blender with the celery cooking liquid, now also cool, together with the rest of the smoked salmon and a few herb leaves for colour and contrast. Add the ricotta or cottage cheese, and blend until smooth.

Sieve or not, as you prefer. Fold in the diced celery and salmon and some more finely chopped herbs. Season with pepper. Whip the cream and fold into the mixture. Whisk the egg whites until stiff but not dry and fold them in. Spoon the mixture into the prepared loaf tin. Cover with clingfilm, and chill in the refrigerator until set. Serve in slices, scoops or quenelles with hot toast, brown bread, crispbreads or slices of grilled polenta.

Vegetable Gratin | serves 8

This is a good-tempered dish that will look after itself in the oven. It is suitable for vegetarians, and is best accompanied by a crisp salad. Double cream or crème fraiche can be used instead of yoghurt, and requires no stabilizing.

450g (1lb) each celeriac, onions, potatoes and leeks
225g (8oz) each fennel or celery and parsnips or Jerusalem artichokes
600ml (1 pint) vegetable stock
1 bay leaf
2 cloves
blade of mace or piece of nutmeg
450ml (¾ pint) thick Greek yoghurt, stabilized by mixing in 1 teaspoon cornflour slaked with 1 tablespoon water and simmered for 5 minutes
6 tablespoons grated cheese
3 tablespoons each ground hazelnuts, rolled oats and fresh breadcrumbs

Peel and slice all the vegetables, the tougher ones about the thickness of a £1 coin, the leeks and artichokes somewhat thicker. Bring the stock and spices to the boil, add the vegetables and cook for 8–10 minutes, adding boiling water if necessary.

Transfer the vegetables to a lightly oiled or buttered baking dish, and reduce the stock by about two-thirds, removing the spices and bay leaf first. Stir in the yoghurt, and cook for 2–3 minutes before pouring over the vegetables. Mix the dry ingredients, and scatter over the top. Bake in a preheated oven at 180°C/350°F/Gas 4 for about 40 minutes.

Root Vegetable Hash with Sausages | serves 4

An inexpensive and easy supper dish, this recipe can be started off on top of the stove, then finished off in the oven. Use a frying pan or oval gratin dish that can go into the oven.

1 celeriac
1 swede
2 turnips
2 medium potatoes
2 parsnips
1 onion
2–3 tablespoons extra virgin olive oil
4 sausages
2 bay leaves or sage leaves
freshly ground black pepper
4 free-range eggs (optional)

Peel and dice the root vegetables quite small, no bigger than 1cm (½in). Peel and chop the onion, and brown it gently in the olive oil before adding the rest of the vegetables. When they are well coated in oil, add the sausages, either whole, cut, or twisted into 2 or 3, or removed from the skin and shaped into patties. Arrange on top of the vegetables. Tuck in the herbs and season lightly with pepper. Bake in a preheated oven at 180–200°C/350–400°F/Gas4–6 for 30–40 minutes. Stir the vegetables from time to time to prevent them from sticking.

If liked, 5–10 minutes before serving, you can make 4 depressions in the vegetables, and slide in the eggs before returning the pan to the oven until the eggs are set. A watercress and orange salad will follow this very well.

Baked and Roasted Vegetables

Roasting in the true sense of the word means cooking on an open fire; baking more correctly describes anything cooked in an enclosed oven. But we still prefer to roast beef and roast potatoes, so here, by extension, are roast vegetables. However, the method of cooking quite removes them from the category of potatoes, cooked around the joint and absorbing fat from it. It is a dish to try when you have the oven on for cooking a pot-roast bird, as these vegetables are marvellous with chicken. Root vegetables contain a good deal of starch, which in cooking turns to sugar, and most spectacularly, when a high heat is applied to cut surfaces which then turn brown, caramelize and seal to give a crisp coating. Half an onion, browned and caramelized in the oven or under the grill, gives an excellent dark colour to stock for casseroles, sauces, and above all, French onion soup.

I use celeriac, parsnips, thick carrots, potatoes, swedes, turnips and sweet potatoes. Apart from the potatoes, I peel the vegetables, and brush the baking dish with olive oil. The vegetables should be cut into wedges to give a large surface area to caramelize. Cook them in a preheated oven at 180–200°C/350–400°/Gas4–6 for about 1 hour. Sweet potatoes should be added about halfway through cooking, as they have a softer flesh.

Braised Fennel Stuffed with Cheese | serves 6

Cooked fennel makes a most versatile dish and can be served as a starter or as a main course as well as a vegetable accompaniment.

6 medium fennel bulbs
3 shallots
55g (2oz) each goat's cheese or blue cheese, hard cheese and soft cheese
a little wine, cider, stock or water

Trim and clean the fennel, and set aside any feathery tops. Cut the bulbs in half vertically. Remove enough of the centre to form a hollow big enough to hold a portion of stuffing. Chop the fennel removed from the centre into tiny dice. Peel and finely chop the shallots. Mix the chopped fennel and shallots with the three cheeses, crumbling the blue cheese and grating the hard cheese.

Drop the fennel halves into a large pan of boiling water, and cook them for 5–10 minutes. Remove and drain them. Divide the stuffing amongst the fennel bulbs, filling the hollows, and place them in a lightly oiled baking dish. Sprinkle with a few drops of wine, cider, stock or water, cover with kitchen foil, and cook in a preheated oven at 190°C/375°F/Gas5, for 15–20 minutes. Timing will depend on the age and freshness of the fennel. It may be done in less than 15 minutes, or take more than 20, if particularly tough and stringy. The fennel can also be sprinkled with breadcrumbs and more grated cheese and baked until golden-brown.

Artichoke, Asparagus and New Potato Casserole in a Butter and Cider Sauce | serves 8

I like to serve this lovely summer vegetable dish on its own rather than as an accompaniment to the main course.

12 tiny or 4 medium artichokes
1kg (2lb) green asparagus
1kg (2lb) new potatoes
85g (3oz) unsalted butter
3 shallots, peeled and finely chopped
5 tablespoons good dry white wine
150ml (¼ pint) dry cider
150ml (¼ pint) vegetable stock or water
6 ripe tomatoes, seeded and chopped
8 basil leaves, torn into shreds
3 tablespoons crème fraiche (optional)
sea salt and freshly ground black pepper
fresh chervil or parsley

If using medium artichokes, pare them right down to the base, and place in a bowl of acidulated water. With tiny artichokes only the outer leaves and the remaining tips need to be removed. Quarter the small artichokes; slice the larger artichoke bottoms into 4–5 pieces, or cut into wedges. Blanch in boiling water for 5 minutes.

Remove and discard any woody stems from the asparagus,

and break into pieces. Blanch the asparagus pieces for 4–5 minutes, and refresh under cold running water. Reserve the tips for garnish. Scrub the potatoes.

In a flameproof casserole melt 25g (1oz) of the butter, and add the shallots, the artichoke pieces and the potatoes, together with the wine and cider. Bring to the boil, and cook briskly for a few minutes. Then add the stock or water, and continue cooking until the vegetables are al dente.

Strain the cooking juices into a pan, boil until reduced by half, then pour it back into the casserole. Add the asparagus pieces, and bring back to the boil. Add the tomatoes and basil, stir in the crème fraiche, if using, and season to taste with salt and pepper. Warm the asparagus tips by pouring boiling water over them. Divide the vegetables among 8 individual dishes and garnish with the asparagus tips and chervil or parsley.

Cauliflower with Beetroot Sauce | serves 4–6

Oriental spices make the most of two of our home-grown vegetables that perhaps do not enjoy the highest culinary reputation.

For the sauce
1 raw beetroot
2–3 tablespoons sherry or cider vinegar
75ml (⅛ pint) walnut oil
sea salt and freshly ground black pepper
pinch of five-spice powder

1 cauliflower
2–3 tablespoons groundnut oil
1 slice of fresh ginger root
1 garlic clove, halved
1 piece of fresh chilli (optional)

If you have a juicer, make the beetroot juice according to the manufacturer's directions. If not, make it in a food processor or blender with a little water, and strain it. Reduce it or not, as you prefer. Whisk the beetroot juice with the vinegar and walnut oil, season to taste with salt, pepper and five-spice powder, and put it to one side while you cook the cauliflower.

Break the cauliflower into florets. The ribs can be used for a soup. Heat the groundnut oil in a wok, together with the ginger, garlic and chilli. When the oil is hot, add the cauliflower, and fry it over a high heat for a few minutes, stirring continuously. It does not matter if it browns a little at the edges, as this gives the finished dish a good flavour, but do not let it burn.

After 4–5 minutes, drain off the oil, and add a little water, just enough to create some steam and stop the cauliflower sticking: about 75ml (3fl oz) is more than enough. Lower the heat, and cover with a lid. Steam for a further 5–8 minutes, or more if you prefer a more tender vegetable. Remove the ginger, garlic and chilli, and season the cauliflower lightly.

Spoon the vinaigrette on to plates, and serve the cauliflower on top. This is good hot, warm, or cold. A garnish of finely shredded preserved or crystallized ginger can be sprinkled on the cauliflower if liked.

Cornish Herb Pie | serves 6–8

Pies and pasties have always been a part of the culinary traditions of the West Country, and this is based on a very old recipe.

450g (1lb) lean green bacon rashers
450g (1lb) leeks, finely chopped
225g (8oz) spinach, finely chopped
55g (2oz) each watercress and parsley, finely chopped
3 free-range eggs
salt and freshly ground black pepper
150ml (¼ pint) chicken stock
225g (8oz) shortcrust pastry
beaten free-range egg and milk, to glaze

Line a 1 litre (2 pint) pie dish with half the bacon rashers, and top with the leeks mixed with the spinach, watercress and parsley. Beat the eggs with the seasoning and stock, and pour over the vegetable mixture.

Lay the remaining bacon rashers on top, and cover with the pastry. Brush with the beaten egg and milk glaze, and bake in a preheated oven at 180°C/350°F/Gas4 for 40–45 minutes, until the pastry is golden-brown.

Herb and Ham Pie | serves 4–6

This recipe is good as a light lunch or supper dish, but is also marvellous for a picnic.

500g (generous 1lb) shortcrust pastry
450g (1lb) gammon or bacon slices
225g (8oz) spinach, washed, blanched and dried
225g (8oz) tender leeks, washed, rinsed, thinly sliced and blanched
bunch of watercress, washed, dried and chopped
chopped fresh chervil
chopped fresh parsley
chopped fresh French tarragon
4 free-range eggs
4 tablespoons cream or stock
freshly ground black pepper
beaten free-range egg and milk, to glaze

Line a pie dish with half the pastry. Cut the gammon or bacon into pieces, and place in the pie. Chop the vegetables and watercress, and mix with a couple of tablespoons of chervil and parsley and rather less of tarragon. Beat the eggs, cream or stock and a little pepper, and pour over the filling.

Roll out the remaining pastry to make a lid. Cover the pie, seal the edges, and brush with the glaze. Place on a baking tray and bake in a preheated oven at 180°C/350°F/Gas4 for 45–60 minutes, until the pastry is golden-brown.

Note

Chicken breasts which have been lightly poached can replace the ham.

Leek, Cauliflower and Blue Cheese Pasties

serves 6

When we filmed at the Mill, there wasn't always food ready by the time we took a break for lunch, and on those days Lostwithiel Bakery came to the rescue, when Tom would drive down for soft baps and Cornish pasties. I liked their vegetable/vegetarian pasties, and they inspired me to devise my own version.

2 medium potatoes, peeled and diced
6–8 leeks, trimmed, cleaned and sliced
½ cauliflower, broken into small florets
250g (9oz) blue cheese (I like to use Beenleigh, Harborne, or Devon Blue, of course)
500g (generous 1lb) shortcrust pastry
freshly ground black pepper
freshly grated nutmeg
sea salt
milk, to glaze

Steam or boil the vegetables until almost tender. Drain and put to one side to cool. Crumble or dice the cheese.

Roll out the pastry, and cut out 6 circles, using a saucer. Pile the vegetables and cheese in the centre of each, and season well with pepper and nutmeg, but only lightly with salt because of the cheese. Wet the pastry rim, fold it over, and seal as for a Cornish pasty.

Brush with milk to glaze, and bake in a preheated oven at 180°C/350°F/Gas4 for 30 minutes.

Serve the pasties hot or warm , although they are very good cold too.

Note

Miniature versions can be made for cocktail snacks.

Fish and Shellfish

Fish

Newlyn is the busiest fishing port and market in England, with each side of the harbour six deep in trawlers at dawn when they are unloading for the early morning auction. The oldest of the piers dates from the Middle Ages, but most were constructed in the second half of the last century.

In 1896 Cornish fishermen rioted here because they objected to east coast trawlers fishing on Sundays, and the militia was called in. The fishing industry has ever been a source of dispute.

John Strike, from the Quayside Fish Centre in Porthleven, buys his fish in Newlyn, where he is regarded as a relatively small purchaser. The big buyers come from Rungis, the wholesale Paris market, and also from the famous Madrid fish market. Outside the market, refrigerated lorries from Spain and France make up the bulk of the carriers, ready to head for the ferry as soon as the auction is over.

Had he been around a hundred years ago, John Strike would have bought much more locally. The harbour in Porthleven, impressively large for so small a town, was built in 1811 to export copper and tin, and bring in mining machinery. He remembers his grandfather describing how the Cornish mackerel boats used to tie up here, and so densely packed were they that you could walk from one side of the harbour to the other, stepping from deck to deck.

Fowey, where we bought much of our fish while living in

the Mill, was the home of the Fowey Gallants, the port's daring sailors, who showed their mettle at the Siege of Calais in 1346, and also built up a reputation as pirates and smugglers. In Cornwall smuggling was also known as fair-trading, a delightful euphemism.

West Country fish is superb, not only the famous Cornish crab and mackerel, but many other varieties besides, and I was also lucky enough to have fish cooked for me on a few occasions when I wasn't working. One night Tom had prepared fillets of Dover sole, and another evening Rick Stein, at the Seafood Restaurant in Padstow, cooked a marvellous dish of plaice and lemon sole in a red wine sauce. And for my own cooking, I found the ugly John Dory quite irresistible, not least for its relatively modest price. I used it in the recipe for Cornish Fish Stew with which I opened the series.

Cornish Fish Stew | serves 4–6

For the stock
1.35–1.8kg (about 3–4lb) fish bones
1 celery stalk
1 slice of fresh ginger root (optional)

For the base
2–3 tablespoons olive oil
1 onion, peeled and chopped
2 leeks, trimmed and sliced
2 celery stalks, trimmed and sliced
4 potatoes, peeled and diced

For the fish
2 red mullet, scaled and cleaned
4 small John Dory, cleaned and trimmed of the fins
1–2 gurnard, cleaned and trimmed of the fins and spines
500g (generous 1lb) pollock or ling, skinned and diced
1 squid, cleaned and cut into rings (optional)

For the herbs and seasonings
fresh parsley
fresh mint
fresh tarragon
fresh coriander
spring onions
sea salt and freshly ground black pepper

Put the fish bones and ginger root, if using, into a saucepan, cover with cold water, simmer for 45–60 minutes, then strain.

To prepare the base, heat the olive oil in a large saucepan, add the vegetables and fry until translucent. Pour on about 600ml (1 pint) fish stock, and cook until the vegetables are tender.

Pour in about 1 litre (2 pints) more stock, and bring to the boil. At this point, add the fish, herbs and seasonings, bring back to simmering point, and cook for 5–8 minutes before serving.

Note

Cider, scrumpy or good dry white wine, can replace at least half the water in the recipe. For a more refined stew, have all the fish carefully filleted, remove the skin from all but the red mullet, and cut into even pieces. This is how we did it when I cooked the fish stew for dinner at the Café Royal Grill Room. As a garnish, we roasted some saffron strands and scattered them over the stew just before serving.

The hot broth quickly unlocked the saffron's fragrance.

Golden Fish Chowder | serves 4–6

Here is another warming fish soup recipe, with a beautiful golden colour from the saffron.

2 tablespoons extra virgin olive oil or butter
1 onion, peeled and chopped
450g (1lb) potatoes, peeled and diced
1.25 litres (about 2 pints) fish stock
pinch of saffron strands
handful of fresh coriander (optional)
1 bay leaf
450g (1lb) undyed smoked haddock fillet
225g (8oz) unsmoked haddock fillet
freshly ground black pepper

Heat the oil or butter in a large saucepan or flameproof oven-to-table casserole, add the onion and potatoes and cook gently without browning until the onion is transparent. Pour on the fish stock, add the saffron, coriander stalks, if using, and bay leaf, and simmer until the potatoes are soft. Remove the herbs.

At this stage you can, if you want a thicker soup, mash some of the potato. Skin the fish fillets and cut into chunks. Put the fish into the soup, and let it barely simmer for 2–3 minutes, until the fish is just cooked through. Season to taste with pepper and stir in the chopped fresh coriander leaves, if using.

To Prepare Cod's Roe

At home as a child, I would watch my father carefully wrap the fragile roe in muslin before lowering it into the pan. This is how my local fishmonger in Hampstead, Andy Theodorou, told me to prepare cod's roe.

Have your fishmonger wrap the roe in two layers of grease-proof, or similar, paper. Keep it in this, and gently lower the parcel into a saucepan of boiling water. Bring back to the boil, lower the heat, and simmer for about an hour.

Allow to cool in the pan, and when you can handle the parcel, unwrap it, and transfer the roe to a shallow dish. Cover with food wrap, weight it, and when cool, refrigerate for a few hours, or until firm.

A pair of roes, joined at one end, weighing about 750–800g (1¾lb) will do for 2–3 meals. Use it sliced in salads, or dip into egg and breadcrumbs, fry and serve with crisp bacon as a good old-fashioned breakfast dish. Or dice and fry it with or without croutons, and use as a filling for a substantial omelette.

Cod's Roe and Smoked Bacon Salad | serves 4

I used to cook this recipe as a weekend treat at the Mill when we were not working, and serve it as a starter.

450g (1lb) cod's roe
8–12 small rashers of rindless, smoked, streaky bacon
55g (2oz) flaked almonds
a generous helping of salad leaves per person
olive oil
cider vinegar or scrumpy

The cod's roe can be cooked the day before required, as described above.

When you are ready to make the salad, fry the bacon until crisp, and remove from the pan. Fry the sliced cod's roe in the bacon fat, together with the almonds. Put the salad leaves on 4 plates, and arrange the cod's roe and bacon on the salad. Scatter on the almonds. Put the pan back on the heat, and pour in some olive oil. Heat, and pour over the salad. Add a tablespoon or two of cider vinegar or scrumpy, and let this boil. Pour it over the salads, and serve immediately.

Chilled Herring Roe Mousse | serves 4

Fragile of texture, delicate of flavour, herring roe is an inexpensive treat. I enjoy it simply dipped in seasoned flour and fried in olive oil, but for a change I like this elegant cold starter.

450g (1lb) cooked herring roe
½ teaspoon grated horseradish
2 tablespoons finely shredded watercress
sea salt and freshly ground black pepper
150ml (¼ pint) double cream, whipped
1 free-range egg white, whisked to peaks

Make a purée of the herring roe and horseradish, then stir in the watercress. Season lightly with salt and pepper, and fold in the whipped cream and whisked egg white. Chill until firmed up, then serve in scoops with hot toast or crusty bread.

Cod Steaks with Bacon and Red Wine Sauce

serves 4

Like all recipes using fish fillets and steaks, these recipes are very quick to cook.

4 cod steaks
8 very thin rashers of rindless smoked or unsmoked streaky bacon
4 tablespoons extra virgin olive oil
freshly ground black pepper
150ml (¼ pint) red wine

Skin the cod steaks, and wrap the bacon rashers around them in place of the skin. Secure with wooden cocktail sticks. Brush the fish all over with olive oil, and use the rest to oil an enamelled gratin dish. Lightly season the fish with pepper, and place in the dish. Pour on the red wine.

Bake in a preheated oven at 190°C/375°F/Gas5 for 10–15 minutes, depending on the thickness of the steaks and how well done you like your fish.

Remove from the oven, and transfer the fish to a warmed serving dish. Cover and keep warm while you boil up and reduce the cooking juices to make the sauce. Serve separately, or poured around the fish, as you wish.

Cod with Grain Mustard Sauce

serves 2,plus leftovers for fish cakes

450–675g (1–1½lb) cod fillet, skinned
1 tablespoon grain mustard
1–2 tablespoons crème fraiche or clotted cream
1 tablespoon finely chopped fresh parsley or watercress
sea salt and freshly ground black pepper

Cut 2 neat, even fillets from the cod, then put all the fish into a non-stick pan. Cover with a lid, and cook over a moderate heat for about 8 minutes, less if the fillet is thin, or you like your fish very lightly cooked, or longer if appropriate. Sweated cod does not sound very nice, but that is what this is. The fish simply cooks in its own juices, releasing some which form the basis of the sauce, without any need for fish stock.

Transfer the fillets to a warmed plate, cover, and keep them warm without allowing them to cook further. Put the fish pieces into a bowl. To make the sauce, stir the mustard, cream and parsley or watercress into the pan juices, raise the heat, and cook for 2–3 minutes until the flavours are well blended. Add salt and pepper, if necessary.

Serve the fish with the sauce and mashed potatoes, of which you should make plenty, in order to have some left over (see below).

Fish Cakes

Mix the remaining fish and mashed potatoes with some more chopped herbs, and, if you like, a little finely chopped shallot or spring onion. Shape into flat cakes, roll in dry breadcrumbs, and refrigerate until required.

For fish cakes, it is best to mash the potatoes without oil or milk; otherwise the mixture is too soft to hold together.

Serve the fish cakes with home-made tomato sauce, or something more exotic like mango chutney into which you have stirred some chopped fresh mint.

Cod with Herb Sauce and Mussels | serves 2

Hake, haddock, ling, pollock, or halibut can be used in the same way.

2 × 175–200g (6–7oz) pieces of cod fillet, or 2 cod cutlets
sea salt and freshly ground black pepper
1 small onion, or 2 shallots, peeled and finely chopped
2 tablespoons extra virgin olive oil
15g (½oz) plain flour
100ml (3½fl oz) hot skimmed or semi-skimmed milk
a good bunch (about 15g (½oz)) of fresh herbs, such as dill, flat-leaf parsley, tarragon and chives
12 large mussels, well scrubbed
4 tablespoons good dry white wine

Season the cod lightly, with salt and pepper and put to one side. Gently cook the onion or shallots in half the olive oil until soft, then make a thick sauce, adding the flour and milk.

While the sauce is cooking, strip the herb leaves from their stems, and chop finely. Put the mussels and white wine into a saucepan, cover and cook until the mussels open. Discard any that do not.

Strain the cooking juices into the sauce, and when the mussels are cool enough to handle, remove from their shells, and put to one side.

Stir the herbs into the sauce. Heat the remaining oil in a

frying pan, or use a non-stick pan and no oil, and fry the cod on both sides until done to your taste, turning it carefully. Stir the mussels into the sauce and spoon it on to the plates, with the fish on top. More herbs can be used to garnish the fish.

If you wish, instead of adding the mussels to the sauce, you can dip them in flour, or in egg and breadcrumbs, and fry them in olive oil.

Smoked Haddock in Saffron, Cider and Herb Sauce | serves 4

450g (1lb) undyed smoked haddock fillet, skinned
150ml (¼ pint) dry or medium-dry cider or scrumpy
pinch of saffron strands
1 tablespoon grain mustard
2 tablespoons clotted cream (optional)
2 tablespoons each chopped fresh chives and parsley
sea salt and freshly ground black pepper

Divide the haddock into 4 even pieces, and put to one side. Put the cider, saffron and mustard into a shallow pan, and bring to the boil. Add the cream, if using, and the herbs, and boil until reduced by about a third.

Put in the fish. Season lightly with salt and pepper. Cover, and remove from the heat. The fish will cook in the residual heat.

I like to serve this with pasta – penne or rigatoni – and combine the freshly cooked, drained pasta with the fish and sauce, stirring it together before serving, which flakes the fish. Alternatively, serve on a bed of rice or mashed potatoes, or with steamed or boiled new potatoes.

Smoked Haddock Salad with Leeks and Oysters in Saffron and Cider Vinaigrette | serves 10

When I cooked a West Country dinner at London's Groucho Club, I wanted to use similar ingredients to those used in the previous recipe, but in a cold starter. This is what I came up with.

1.35kg (3lb) undyed smoked haddock, filleted, skinned and portioned
600ml (1 pint) dry or medium-dry cider
good pinch of saffron strands
2 tablespoons grain mustard
2 tablespoons each chopped fresh chives and parsley
sea salt and freshly ground black pepper
cider vinegar
extra virgin olive oil
salad leaves
steamed leeks
10 rock oysters, poached

Poach the fish very lightly in the cider with the saffron and mustard. Remove the fish and boil the liquor until reduced by about a half. Add the herbs, seasoning, extra saffron, a dash of cider vinegar and olive oil, to make a vinaigrette. Put salad leaves on 10 serving plates, and place the fish on top and a few leeks around. Place an oyster on top of each serving of fish and splash on the dressing.

Skate Salad with Apple and Bacon | serves 4–6

Skate is an underrated fish. I love its texture and flavour, on or off the bone. It is particularly good when matched with sharp-tasting dressings or sauces, as in this and the following recipe.

675g (1½lb) skate wing
600ml (1 pint) cider
sea salt and freshly ground black pepper
salad leaves
2 crisp apples
2 tablespoons cider vinegar
4 rashers of rindless smoked streaky bacon
4 tablespoons apple juice

Poach the skate in the cider, seasoned with a little salt and pepper, for about 5–8 minutes. Remove from the heat, and allow to cool. Put the salad leaves on serving plates.

Quarter, core and thinly slice the apple, and toss in the vinegar to prevent browning. Cut the bacon into thin strips. Fry them in a pan until the fat runs and the pieces are crisp.

Remove the skate from the cartilage, and put on top of the salad leaves. Arrange the apple slices and crisp bacon pieces on top. Heat the pan, and pour the hot bacon fat over the salad. Deglaze the pan with apple juice, and pour it over the salad.

Note

If you prefer not to use bacon, fry some pine kernels or almond flakes in a little olive oil instead.

Warm Skate with Saffron Vinaigrette | serves 4

450–675g (1–1½lb) skate wing

For the vinaigrette
pinch of saffron strands, soaked in boiling water
6 tablespoons extra virgin olive oil
sea salt and freshly ground black pepper
1 tablespoon sherry vinegar, lemon or orange juice

Mix the vinaigrette ingredients and leave for the flavours to develop while you poach, steam or bake the skate, according to your chosen method, allowing 8–10 minutes depending on thickness.

Discard the skin, then remove the fish from the cartilage. Heap on to plates, on a bed of salad leaves or thinly sliced and degorged cucumber, if you wish, and spoon over the vinaigrette.

Baked Mackerel with Fennel and Gooseberry Sauce | serves 4

This and the next recipe are for early summer, when the first of the gooseberries are available.

4 mackerel, cleaned and gutted, heads and backbone removed
extra virgin olive oil
sea salt and freshly ground black pepper
4 tablespoons cider
225g (8oz) gooseberries
1 fennel bulb, chopped
55g (2oz) butter, cut into small cubes

Brush the mackerel with olive oil, season with salt and pepper and sprinkle with cider. Oil an ovenproof dish, and place the fish in it. Bake in a preheated oven at 180°C/350°F/Gas 4 for about 20 minutes.

Meanwhile, make the sauce: cook the gooseberries and fennel until soft in just enough water to prevent them from burning. When soft, sieve into a saucepan. Drain in any cooking juices from the fish, and reheat. Beat in the butter until well mixed, and serve with the fish.

Mackerel and New Potatoes with Walnut and Gooseberry Vinaigrette | serves 6

3 mackerel, filleted, and each fillet cut into 3
sea salt and freshly ground black pepper
2 shallots, peeled and finely chopped
900g (2lb) new potatoes, scrubbed and freshly boiled

For the vinaigrette
1 tablespoon chopped fresh chervil, parsley, or herb fennel
75ml (⅛ pint) walnut oil
2–3 tablespoons gooseberry vinegar (see page 314)

Heat a non-stick frying pan, and in it fry the mackerel pieces, skin side first until crisp and golden-brown, lightly seasoning the top surface. Turn the fish quickly and cook for just long enough to colour the uncooked surface.

Arrange on a platter, skin side up. Mix the shallots and new potatoes with the vinaigrette and herbs. Serve with the mackerel.

Sardines 'en Papillote' | serves 4

4–8 fresh sardines
juice and thinly pared zest of 1 lime
sea salt and freshly ground black pepper
extra virgin olive oil

Scale and rinse the sardines, and cut off their heads. Cut them open down the belly, gut, rinse and open out. Strip the backbone at the tail end, and carefully lift out, removing as many of the smaller bones as possible.

Brush with lime juice, season with salt and pepper, and sprinkle with olive oil. Place a strip of lime zest inside each fish and close up.

Brush 4 circles of greaseproof paper with oil. Put one or two sardines on one half of each greaseproof circle. Fold over, and fold and twist the edges together to seal tightly.

Place on a baking sheet, and bake in a preheated oven at 180°C/350°F/Gas4 for 10–12 minutes.

Note

Other fish can of course be cooked in the same way – red mullet, for example, or fillets of sole or plaice, or pieces of cod or haddock. It is a simple, quick cooking method which retains the full flavour of the fish. Instead of paper, you can cut circles of filo dough, using two for each envelope, brushing each with melted butter, and sealing the fish into the circles of dough before baking at the same temperature for the same time.

Baked Sardines with Mint and Cider | serves 4

8–12 sardines, depending on size
75 ml (⅛ pint) good dry cider
sea salt and freshly ground black pepper
1 tablespoon finely chopped fresh mint
3 tablespoons fresh breadcrumbs
2 tablespoons extra virgin olive oil
lemon wedges, to serve

For the garnish
fresh mint or flat-leaf parsley

Ask your fishmonger to scale, gut, and remove the heads from the sardines, or do this yourself.

Arrange the sardines in an oiled baking dish. Pour on the cider, and season lightly with salt and pepper. Mix the mint with the breadcrumbs, spoon over the fish and press down. Sprinkle with the olive oil.

Bake in a preheated oven at 190°C/375°F/Gas 5 for 10 minutes. Serve with lemon wedges and garnish with fresh mint leaves or flat-leaf parsley.

Grey Mullet Baked with Fennel and Mint

serves 4–6

I first developed this recipe in my parents' kitchen in Gozo, where we cooked grouper. The flavours of mint and fennel, however, lend themselves equally to grey mullet, or indeed any whole fish, such as sea bream, sea bass and salmon trout.

about 1.1–1.35kg (2½–3lb) grey mullet
1 medium onion, peeled and thinly sliced
several sprigs of fresh mint
handful of fresh herb fennel, or 1 fennel bulb, thinly sliced
½ bottle good dry white wine
2 tablespoons extra virgin olive oil
sea salt and freshly ground black pepper

Make sure the fish is scaled, gutted and cleaned. Rinse thoroughly under cold running water, and dry with kitchen paper. Lightly oil a roasting tin or a long ovenproof dish. Lay some of the onion on the bottom, place some inside the fish cavity, and save the rest to lay on top. Reserve the tops of the mint sprigs and some of the fennel for garnish, and divide the rest between the bottom of the dish, the fish cavity and the top of the fish. Pour the wine over the fish in the baking dish, and sprinkle on the oil.

Season lightly with salt and pepper, cover loosely with kitchen foil and bake in a preheated oven at 180°C/350°F/

Gas4 for about 1 hour. An exact cooking time cannot be given because much depends on the thickness of the fish at its thickest part. Some like their fish well cooked, others prefer it just slightly translucent in the centre. Generally I follow the Canadian rule and allow 10 minutes per 2.5cm (1in).

Transfer the fish, when cooked, to a serving platter. Cover to keep it warm, but do not let it cook further. Pour the herbs, cooking juices and onion into a saucepan, bring to the boil, add more seasoning, if necessary, and rub through a fine sieve around the fish. Garnish with the reserved mint and fennel. Fish cooked in this way is very good with boiled or steamed potatoes.

Fish Baked in a Salt Crust | serves 4

This is another recipe I learned to cook in a much warmer climate, where sea salt is cheap because the summers are hot enough to evaporate seawater, leaving behind glistening piles of crystalline sea salt. A rather less expensive version for our own climate mixes sea salt with flour to make a dough. The flavour and juice of the fish are hermetically sealed, and only released when the crust is cut open at the table.

about 1–1.5kg (2½–3lb) salmon trout, sea bass, snapper or bream scaled and cleaned, but left whole
3 bay leaves

For the salt crust
450g (1lb) plain flour
225g (8oz) coarse salt
grated zest of 1 lemon
small sprigs of fresh thyme
3 free-range egg whites
225ml (8fl oz) water

First make the salt crust: either by hand, or in a food processor, mix together the dry ingredients. Beat together the egg whites and water, and mix into the flour and salt to form a firm dough. It should not be sticky, but if it is, add a little flour, and if too dry, add more water: not more than a tablespoon of either should be needed. Knead the dough until smooth, cover, and let it rest for half an hour or so.

Roll the dough out to a rectangle large enough to enclose the fish, and place on a baking sheet. Put a bay leaf in the fish cavity, one on top of the dough and one on top of the fish. Fold one long side of dough over the fish, and brush the edge with water. Bring the other side of the dough up to the middle, and pinch to seal it. Pinch the ends. Bake in a preheated oven at 200–220°C/400–425°F/Gas 6–7 for 35 minutes for a 1.1kg (2½lb) fish, and an extra 5 minutes for each extra 450g (1lb).

Remove from the oven, and leave for 10–20 minutes. It will stay very hot for at least half an hour.

Cut open the fish at the table and serve it filleted, with a few steamed, boiled or baked new potatoes and some simple sauces, such as melted butter, lemon juice and finely chopped fresh parsley, extra virgin olive oil with crushed garlic and fresh coriander, and a light mayonnaise flavoured with grated orange zest, orange juice and finely chopped fresh chives.

Wild Salmon in Cider | serves 6–8

In June you might be lucky enough to get Tamar salmon. Try Lloyd Downes's stall in Plymouth's Pannier Market for it. This and the following four recipes make the most of this lovely fish.

about 1.5kg (generous 3lb) middle cut salmon or salmon fillet
85g (3oz) butter
salt and freshly ground black pepper
freshly grated nutmeg
2 small shallots, peeled and chopped
1 teaspoon chopped fresh parsley
150ml (¼ pint) cider

Clean and wash the salmon, cut it into 3–4 equal portions, and place in a well-buttered ovenproof dish. Season with salt, pepper and nutmeg. Sprinkle the salmon with the shallots and parsley, and dot with butter. Moisten with cider. Bake in a preheated oven at 190°C/375°F/Gas 5, basting frequently, for about 12–15 minutes, or until just cooked.

Souchy of Wild Salmon | serves 4

450–675g (1–1½lb) wild salmon fillet
sea salt and freshly ground black pepper
salmon bones and head
1 celery stalk
parsley stalks
fresh chives
fresh tarragon stalks or lovage
850ml (1½ pints) dry white wine

For the garnish
fresh tarragon or lovage leaves

Slice the salmon very thinly, season with salt and pepper, and put to one side. Make a broth with the remaining ingredients, simmer for 30–40 minutes and sieve.

Have the soup plates very hot, and lay the salmon pieces in them with the herbs on top. Pour the boiling broth over the salmon, and serve immediately.

Midsummer Salmon with a Herb Tapestry

serves 4–6

1kg (generous 2lb) wild salmon fillet, skin and bones removed
55g (2oz) unsalted butter, softened
sea salt and freshly ground black pepper
fresh chervil
fresh basil
fresh tarragon
fresh flat-leaf parsley
2–3 tablespoons dry cider

Spread the fish all over with the butter, and season it lightly with salt and pepper. Strip the herb leaves from their stems, and place all over the fish, the butter helping to anchor the leaves. Put the cider into a roasting bag, then add the piece of fish. Secure the bag tightly, having expelled all the air.

Have a very large pot or fish kettle of boiling water ready, and submerge the parcel of fish in it. Allow to come back to simmering point, and cook the fish for 5 minutes. Remove the pan from the heat, leaving the fish to cook in its bag in the water.

Remove when at room temperature, and serve with a salad of new potatoes and a green leaf salad.

Drain off the cooking juices, reduce, and use to flavour a mayonnaise or a sauce made simply of crème fraiche.

Salmon Tartare with Cucumber Sauce

serves 4 as a starter

350g (12oz) wild salmon, skinned
1 shallot, peeled and finely chopped (optional)
2 tablespoons extra virgin olive oil
salt and freshly ground black pepper
1–2 ripe tomatoes
1 cucumber
1 teaspoon grated horseradish
1 tablespoon cream, thick yoghurt or buttermilk

Chop the salmon into very small pieces. If you prefer to use a food processor, process very briefly, otherwise salmon paste will be the result. Mix the shallot, if using, with the salmon, together with a spoonful of olive oil. Season lightly with salt and pepper. Cover and put to one side.

Skin and halve the tomatoes. Scoop the seeds and pulp into a sieve set over a bowl, and rub through the liquid. Cut the tomatoes into strips or dice for garnish. Peel and halve the cucumber, remove the seeds, and chop or slice. Fry the cucumber in the remaining oil for 5–6 minutes, then put into a blender or food processor with the horseradish and cream. Blend until smooth.

Mix the salmon with enough of the tomato liquid to add a slight note of acidity, and spoon on to plates, or shape using ring moulds. Spoon the sauce around it, and add the tomato for garnish.

Potted Salmon

An excellent way of using up cooked salmon, this is better not made in a food processor, which turns it into salmon paste. I prefer the slightly uneven texture achieved when making it by hand. Use equal quantities of butter and cooked salmon, or slightly more fish, depending on your taste. Season the fish lightly with salt and pepper, and pull it apart with two forks until you have a pile of shreds. Either clarified or very soft butter can be used: stir it into the salmon until well mixed. Season to taste, adding mace or nutmeg if liked, and pot in a jar or ramekins. Top with clarified butter if planning to keep it for a few days in the refrigerator. Cooked, undyed smoked haddock is also very good prepared in this way.

To clarify butter

As this is butter with its moisture removed, it keeps well in the refrigerator and is worth making in reasonable quantity. Melt the butter slowly in a heavy saucepan so that it does not burn. Line a sieve with a damp muslin cloth, and carefully pour the butter through it, keeping back as much of the milky sediment as possible. When the sieved butter has settled, but before it solidifies, pour it once more through the sieve and into a container for storing. When using to cover a pot of pâté, only melt as much as you need.

Baked Stuffed Sea Trout | serves 4–6

about 1.5kg (generous 3lb) sea trout, scaled, cleaned, gutted and boned
juice of 1 lemon
sea salt and freshly ground black pepper
4 slices of white bread, crusts removed, soaked in milk and then squeezed
6 anchovy fillets, chopped
175g (6oz) shelled prawns, chopped
115g (4oz) unsalted butter, softened
2 free-range hard-boiled eggs, chopped
¼ teaspoon ground mace
2 tablespoons chopped fresh chives or spring onion
150ml (¼ pint) good dry white wine

Season the fish inside and out with lemon juice, salt and pepper. Mix together all the remaining ingredients, except the wine and half the butter. Stuff the fish with the mixture and secure with wooden cocktail sticks.

Place the fish in a buttered dish, pour on the wine, cover with kitchen foil, and cook in a preheated oven at 170°C/325°F/Gas3 for 50–60 minutes. Transfer the fish to a serving platter, reduce the cooking juices, and hand separately. Salmon and rainbow trout can be cooked in the same way.

This baked salmon trout can be served with new potatoes

and a dish of lightly cooked cucumber, a perfect accompaniment to this and the previous cooked salmon dishes.

Cold Poached Fish in Jelly

On the subject of hot summer days, here is a marvellously versatile recipe for fish set in a crystal-clear and flavoursome jelly. In many ways, it is the summer version of the Cornish fish stew with which this chapter opened.

whole fish, steaks or fillets (see below)
4 leaves of gelatine or 4 teaspoons powdered gelatine per 600ml (1 pint) court bouillon (see below)

For the court bouillon
600ml (1 pint) good dry white wine
600ml (1 pint) water
1 celery stalk, chopped
1 slice of fresh ginger root (optional)
1 strip of orange zest
2 bay leaves
1 sprig each of fresh tarragon and thyme
handful of parsley stalks
1 teaspoon peppercorns
2 teaspoons salt

First make the court bouillon: simmer all the ingredients in a saucepan for 30 minutes. Strain into a wide, shallow pan, such as a sauteuse, or frying pan, and bring to the boil.

Carefully lower the fish into the boiling court bouillon,

which will immediately go off the boil. Lower the heat, and bring the liquid gently back to just under simmering point, where the water shivers but no bubbles break the surface. Thick fish steaks should be poached for about 10 minutes; fillets or skate wings are poached for about 5–8 minutes, and whole fish, such as salmon or sea bass, for 10 minutes for each 2.5cm (1in) thickness at the thickest part (i.e. the shoulder).

Remove the fish carefully, and drain it on a clean towel or kitchen paper, then transfer to a rack to cool. If poaching a very large fish, you will need to make double or triple the quantity of court bouillon.

To make 600ml (1 pint) jelly, strain the cooking liquid through a sieve lined with wet muslin. Measure out just over 450ml (¾ pint), and pour into a jug. Soften the gelatine in just under 150ml (¼ pint) cold water in a bowl. Stir the softened gelatine into the hot liquid until it has dissolved. Season the liquid to taste, bearing in mind that as it cools, the flavour will weaken. Leave to become cold. Lay the fish in a terrine, ring mould, jelly mould or soup plates. Add any herbs, spices or other garnish, and spoon on the cold liquid. Cover carefully and refrigerate until set.

Note

The court bouillon can be flavoured with a saffron liquid made by infusing a pinch of saffron strands in 3–4 tablespoons of court bouillon.

Suggested combinations

Skate shreds and salmon cubes with skinned, seeded and diced tomatoes set in a saffron jelly.

Salmon and scallops with sliced or diced cucumber, degorged first, set in a mint jelly made by infusing mint leaves in court bouillon. Add whole mint leaves to the jelly.

Prawns with halibut, cod or monkfish with chopped fresh dill set in a dill and lemon jelly.

Shellfish

In 1839 Mr Justice Coleridge sentenced three men for oyster stealing. A copy of his judgement hangs in the Shipwright's Arms, Helford's only pub, and serves as a warning even today to those who covet the contents of the Duchy oyster beds looked after by Len Hodges and his son Lindsey.

> The owner of a fishery must be as safe in the enjoyment and possession of his property as the owner of a house. He is paying a rent of £450 a year for the enjoyment of all this. How is he to pay the rent if all people are to go and take away the oysters, and if one can do so others may do it. You have no more right to do that than you have to go into a field and take a sheep.

The sentence was six weeks' hard labour for all three.

Daphne du Maurier in *Frenchman's Creek* describes the Helford river and its wooded brown creeks much better than I can. One of the first things I did when I got to Cornwall was hunt out a second-hand copy of this most romantic of novels, and very soon I found it in Falmouth. I opened it at page one and read,

> When the east wind blows up Helford river the shining waters become troubled and disturbed and the little waves beat angrily upon the sandy shores. The short seas break

above the bar at ebbtide, and the waders fly inland to the mud-flats, their wings skimming the surface, and calling to one another as they go. Only the gulls remain, wheeling and crying above the foam, diving now and again in search of food, their grey feathers glistening with the salt spray.

The long rollers of the channel, travelling from beyond Lizard Point, follow hard upon the steep seas at the river mouth, and mingling with the surge and wash of deep sea water comes the brown tide, swollen with the last rains and brackish from the mud, bearing upon its face dead twigs and straws, and strange forgotten things, leaves too early fallen, young birds, and the buds of flowers.

The open roadstead is deserted, for an east wind makes uneasy anchorage, and but for the few houses scattered here and there above Helford passage, and the group of bungalows about Port Navas, the river would be the same as it was in a century now forgotten, in a time that has left few memories.

The Helford river estuary today is little different from that description, still a maze of peaceful tree-lined creeks of dark still water. Port Navas is one of these creeks, the setting for a small village of stone cottages and the oyster fisheries of the Duchy of Cornwall. Said to date back to Roman times, the oysters – the native oyster, *ostrea edulis* – grow in beds marked by 'withies' or narrow stakes. They used to be the food of the poor who gathered them in the mud-banks of the creek. Sam

Weller in Dickens' *Pickwick Papers* says: 'It's a wery remarkable circumstance that poverty and oysters go together.'

Not any more. Native oysters cost about £1.50 each in our local fishmongers, if we are lucky enough to find them. They take about five years to grow to maturity, compared to the two and a half years needed by the fast-growing Pacific oysters.

From Port Navas, as I stood on the shingle at low tide, I could see Frenchman's Creek, grey and bleak in the rain and not the dreamy, romantic stretch of water, almost enclosed in its leafy arbour of overhanging trees where the Frenchman hid his boat. I left the river bank and went indoors to help Lindsey Hodge grade the oysters he was about to send up to London.

The Hodges also receive visitors who come to buy direct. When the weather is fine, Len might be persuaded to open their oysters and they will picnic right there by the river. Despite the piercing cold and driving rain, we also had a picnic: oysters, brown bread and butter and Guinness. That truly is a meal to be remembered – and the combination of Guinness and oysters is hard to beat.

Oysters were formerly used much more extensively in English cookery, when their cost permitted it. Mutton and oyster pudding was a favourite in Victorian times: a pudding basin was lined with suet pastry, filled with sliced or diced lean mutton, and a few oysters pushed into the centre. After the pudding had steamed for 4 hours, a hole was made in the suet crust and the oyster liquor poured in.

Mrs Beeton has a lovely recipe in which oysters are stuffed

inside a young chicken, which is then poached. The cooking juices are reduced, flavoured with mace, enriched with cream and egg yolks, and at the end, a few more oysters are added to the sauce.

I, too, like to combine oysters with meat, although I will usually use the less expensive Pacific oyster, and am particularly partial to my oyster hamburger. Much unpleasant food masquerades under the name of hamburger, which is sad, for a real hamburger, made with good-quality, lean, flavoursome beef, is a treat. It may not qualify as a 'serious' meal, with a beginning, middle and end, but, set against the realities of modern life, it makes a perfect snack, a lunchtime sandwich, something at the end of a busy day, especially for just one or two people. A hidden filling of oysters turns the hamburger into a feast. It is a fast and modern interpretation of the carpetbag steak, a juicy fillet stuffed with raw oysters and grilled.

Oyster-stuffed Hamburgers

For each hamburger you need:

115g (4oz) trimmed lean beef
1½–2 teaspoons trimmed and finely chopped shallots (optional)
1 teaspoon finely chopped fresh herbs (optional)
pinch of freshly ground black pepper
sea salt
3–4 shucked oysters
1 bun

Mince or finely chop the beef. Mix the meat with the shallots, herbs and pepper, and shape into a firm, neat patty shape, roughly the size of the bun, ensuring that the oysters are enclosed in the meat. Have the grill hot, or use a well-seasoned cast-iron or non-stick frying pan.

Cook the hamburger on both sides until done to your liking. Lightly salt it, and serve hot on a lightly toasted soft bap. Have all your accompaniments ready before you start.

Veal and Oyster Collops | serves 8

Here is a similar recipe, for which I use free-range veal when I can get it. Otherwise use lamb fillet or fillet of beef.

1kg (generous 2lb) fillet of veal
16 fresh oysters
seasoned plain flour
1 egg
dried breadcrumbs
55g (2oz) butter

For the garnish
lemon slices

Cut the veal into 8 equal slices, each about 2cm (¾ in) thick. Remove the oysters from their shells, and reserve the liquid. Cut a slit in each piece of veal with the point of a sharp knife, and stuff with 2 oysters. Dust with seasoned flour, brush with beaten egg, and coat with breadcrumbs. Fry in butter until the meat is tender and the outside golden-brown.

Make a gravy with the pan juices and the reserved oyster liquid. Pour over the veal, and garnish with lemon slices.

Potato and Oyster Pie | serves 6–8

I devised this recipe many years ago after visiting an oyster farm in Tamales Bay, northern California. It is equally good with Helford river oysters.

115g (4oz) butter, plus extra for greasing
1.5kg (generous 3lb) waxy potatoes
450g (1lb) fresh spinach leaves
sea salt and freshly ground black pepper
cayenne pepper
1.25 litres (2 pints) shucked oysters plus the juice, carefully sieved
6 sheets of filo pastry

Butter a deep, rectangular ovenproof dish. Scrub and parboil the potatoes until just yielding and tender. When cool enough to handle, peel and thinly slice them. Wash the spinach in several changes of water, and remove the central stems if tough. Blanch the spinach by draping the leaves, if they are large, over a colander and pouring boiling water over them. If small, put them into a large pan of boiling water, keep on the boil for a minute, then drain, rinse and thoroughly dry them.

Arrange a thick layer of potatoes in the bottom of the dish. Season lightly with salt and pepper, including the cayenne. Spread half the spinach leaves over the potatoes, and dot with a quarter of the butter. Arrange the oysters on the spinach, and cover with the remaining spinach, a little more butter, the rest of the potatoes, more butter and seasoning, and finally sprinkle the oyster juices over the potatoes. Top with 6 sheets of filo pastry, each one brushed with melted butter and laid on separately. Tuck the edges of the pastry inside the rim of the dish, and bake in the centre of a preheated oven at 190°C/375°F/Gas 5 for 40–45 minutes.

Potato and Mussel Salad | serves 6

Steaming is a good way of cooking this recipe. If you have a tiered steamer, the potatoes can be put on to steam first and the mussels added to the next tier for the last few minutes. Small, waxy potatoes and mussels, bound with a creamy dressing or mayonnaise, are a marvellous combination. Serve it as a starter or as part of a large buffet.

900g (2lb) waxy, firm potatoes
1.5kg (generous 3lb) mussels
300ml (½ pint) soured cream, single cream or homemade mayonnaise
lemon juice to taste
sea salt and freshly ground black pepper
fresh chives, dill or parsley

Scrub and steam the potatoes for about 15 minutes. Meanwhile, scrub and rinse the mussels, discarding any that remain open. (Mussels now generally come without barnacles, but if any are encrusted, then knock them off with the back of an old knife.) Place the mussels in a steamer basket on top of the potatoes or in a separate steamer over a high heat. Cover and steam for a few minutes until the shells open. Discard any that do not.

When cool enough to handle, remove the mussels from their shells and put them into a bowl. Skin or peel the potatoes, if you wish, and dice or slice them. Mix them with the mussels. When somewhat cooler, mix them with the dressing. If mayonnaise is used and the potatoes are too hot, this will cause the mayonnaise to split. Snip up the herbs, and fold into the salad. This is very good freshly made, still tepid, rather than from the refrigerator.

Skewers of Mussels and Oysters | serves 4

Barbecue weather does not usually coincide with an 'r' in the month, when native oysters are in season, but you can use the less expensive Pacific oysters.

4 rashers of rindless streaky bacon
24 large mussels
8 Pacific oysters
85g (3oz) unsalted butter, melted
100g (3½oz) fresh breadcrumbs

Blanch the bacon in boiling water for 2 minutes. Clean the mussels as described in the previous recipe. Steam the mussels until they are just open, and remove from the shells when cool enough to handle. Discard any mussels that do not open.

Remove the oysters from their shells, using a special oyster knife: wrap your hand holding the oyster in a tea-towel, in case the knife should slip, and insert the point between the 2 halves of the shell, then prise open. Cut each rasher of bacon into 3–4 pieces, and thread on 4 skewers with alternating shellfish.

Roll the full skewers in melted butter and breadcrumbs, and grill for 5–8 minutes, turning from time to time.

Serve the skewers alone, or on a bed of salad with a lemony vinaigrette.

Mussels in Scrumpy

serves 2 as a main course, 4 as a starter

A version of *moules marinière* was cooked in England in the Middle Ages using beer. The dish works equally well with cider or scrumpy.

about 2kg (generous 4lb) mussels
1 small onion, peeled and finely chopped
2 celery stalks, trimmed and finely sliced
1 leek, trimmed and thinly sliced
1 carrot, peeled and grated
½ teaspoon freshly ground black pepper
300ml (½ pint) dry or medium-dry scrumpy

Scrub the mussels under cold running water, and remove the beards and any barnacles. Discard any open (dead) mussels. Put the vegetables, pepper and scrumpy into a heavy-lidded flameproof casserole, bring to the boil, cover, and simmer for a few minutes until the vegetables are tender. Open the casserole, tip in the well-rinsed mussels, and put the lid back on. Give the casserole a vigorous shake or two to distribute the vegetables and seasoning.

Let the mussels steam for 5 minutes or so. Serve from the pot with bread to mop up the juices. A dollop of clotted cream can be added to enrich the sauce.

Little Oyster Pies | makes 6

This is one of my very favourite recipes for canapés or hot hors d'œuvres. You can also use mussels, opening them as described on page 107.

6 blanched spinach leaves
175g (6oz) flaky or shortcrust pastry
egg yolk beaten with water, to glaze (optional)

For the filling
6 oysters
freshly ground black pepper
85g (3oz) butter, softened
3 anchovy fillets, chopped
good pinch of ground mace
2 tablespoons fresh white breadcrumbs
grated zest of ½ lemon
a little lemon juice

Remove the oysters from their shells, keeping the juice. Season lightly with pepper. Mix the remaining ingredients, together with the strained oyster juice, and wrap each oyster and a little stuffing in a spinach leaf. Roll out the pastry, and line 6 tart tins. Cut the rest of the pastry into 6 circles for the lids.

Place some of the remaining stuffing mixture in the lined tart tins, place the wrapped oysters on top and cover with the remaining butter mixture. Top the tarts with pastry lids. Brush with an egg yolk and water glaze if you wish, and bake in a preheated oven at 200°C/400°F/Gas 6 for 10 minutes. Serve hot or warm.

Note

Alternatively, cut out circles of pastry and make oyster pasties.

Barbecued Oysters | serves 6

If you have always had problems opening oysters, let the barbecue do it for you. This is a marvellous way of cooking oysters in the summer, especially for a party. You can put the sauce ingredients on a convenient table and let everyone dip their own oysters once cooked on the coals. You will hear the oysters creak a little as the shells begin to part and they will be perfectly – cooked, I was going to say, but the heat does nothing more than 'set' them.

2–3 dozen Pacific oysters

Scrub the oysters, and place them flat shell down on the grill for 5 minutes. Turn them over, and leave, flat shell uppermost, until the shell begins to creak and open slightly. Wear thick gloves when you remove the oysters, and then, with an oyster knife, give a helping hand, a final twist to remove the top shell. A little sauce is spooned on to the oyster before eating it.

Sauce suggestions

English: melted butter, lemon juice, white pepper, chopped fresh tarragon

Oriental: crushed salted black beans (available from oriental supermarkets), chopped chillies, chopped spring onions, rice vinegar, rice wine (or sherry vinegar and dry sherry), toasted sesame oil, soy sauce

Mediterranean: extra virgin olive oil, finely chopped garlic, chopped black olives, finely chopped basil, finely chopped sun-dried or fresh tomatoes

Classical: red wine vinegar, finely chopped shallots, freshly ground pepper

Scallop and Saffron Griddle Cakes | makes 12–16

Scallops are usually such a rare treat that I like to serve them just grilled or steamed. But should they be plentiful, here is an unusual way of preparing them. They are very good served with a dollop of soured cream into which you have snipped some chives or spring onions, and perhaps some green chilli.

pinch of saffron strands, soaked in hot water
115g (4oz) plain flour
1 free-range egg
about 150ml (¼ pint) buttermilk or plain yoghurt thinned down with water
2 scant teaspoons baking powder
225g (8oz) queen scallops
sea salt and freshly ground black pepper
snipped fresh chives, chervil or parsley
oil, or butter for frying

Beat the saffron water, flour, egg and buttermilk or yoghurt together to form a thick batter. Heat a frying pan, lightly greased with oil or butter, and just before you are ready to cook, sprinkle the baking powder into the batter and beat again thoroughly. Then stir in the scallops, seasoning and herbs. If the scallops are on the large side, halve or quarter them.

Pour a small ladle of batter into the pan. Do *not* shake the pan to spread the mixture: these should be small, quite thick cakes. You will probably be able to cook 4 at a time. When the top surface looks matt and full of holes, flip the cakes over to cook the underside for 2–3 minutes. Serve them hot or warm.

Note

Clams, cockles, whitebait, oysters or mussels can replace the scallops.

Crab and Lobster

Crab was my lunch of choice when we broke from filming on location, and I always looked forward to the quayside inn in Falmouth, Penzance or wherever we found ourselves, and ordered some local draught bitter, such as Sharp's of Wadebridge, to go with a real doorstep of a sandwich, several inches thick with crab.

When the crabs are at their biggest, best and least expensive, have a change from crab salad and try a traditional crab soup. But perhaps we should first consider whether to buy the crab ready-cooked or do it ourselves. One summer I spent a good deal of time researching the subject, as well as dealing with the practical aspect.

Cooking Crab and Lobster

I have come to the conclusion that to get the freshest, sweetest product, you should cook the crustacean yourself if possible, rather than buying them ready-cooked. Lobster in particular is an expensive ingredient, and it is worth eating it as its very best.

However, cooking it yourself means killing it yourself. A crab has two nerve centres, and these should be destroyed before the creature is cooked. RSPCA advice is to use an awl or something pointed of similar diameter. Turn the crab on to its back, lift the tail flap, and you will see a small hole at the base of a distinct groove. Paralyse the crab by firmly piercing this nerve centre to a depth of at least 1cm (½in). Complete the process by pushing the awl or skewer between the movable plates at the mouth, between the eyes. The crab can then be boiled or steamed.

According to the RSPCA, there is no known way of killing lobsters absolutely humanely, and if there is any uncertainty, the creature should have the benefit of the doubt. Some people suggest electrically stunning lobsters; others recommend putting them into lukewarm salt water and very gradually raising the heat. A short, sharp blow through the nervous system has its advocates too. But in Canada and Maine, lobsters are plunged into an inch or two of fast-boiling water. 'Live crustaceans die in a few seconds,' we are told by a number of cookery experts. According to the RSPCA, it can take 2–3 minutes, rather than a few seconds, for a lobster to die in boiling water. If a large number of crustaceans are being cooked in a big pot, then it can take much longer because the water will take much longer to come back to the boil. And boiling water is in any case, of course, completely alien to the lobster's natural environment.

Lobsters live in very cold water, and the RSPCA recommends, as the least inhumane way of killing them, and the one most feasible for a domestic kitchen, chilling the lobster in ice slurry, or in the freezer for about 30 minutes, which reduces it to a state of torpor. It is then killed by piercing it through the cross mark in the carapace, with a heavy cleaver or kitchen knife, cutting right down to the chopping board. The lobster can then be boiled or steamed. For steaming or grilling, it can be split right down the middle if you wish, and opened out. All that needs removing are the feathery gills under the carapace, the stomach sac or gritty substance in the 'head' part of the lobster and the intestine, which runs down the middle of the tail and is quite visible when the lobster is split down the middle. Severing through the nerve system with a heavy knife or cleaver is indeed the fastest and most efficient way to kill a lobster, if you are deft with these implements. It is the method used by many chefs.

Cooking times: Once the water has come back to the boil, allow 15–20 minutes for a 900g–1.5kg (2–3lb) crab. Canadian and Maine lobsters have a thinner shell than the Scottish or European lobster. The usual size is about 600g (1¼ lb). Allow 12 minutes for a Canadian lobster and 15 for a European lobster, once the water has come back to the boil. The shell of a European lobster is a much more defined, dark-blue colour, whereas the Canadian lobster shell is greenish-brown. Both, of course, turn bright red when cooked. After experimenting with both kinds, I have come to the conclusion that, like most things, lobsters are a matter of taste. Whilst I found both Canadian and European, when bought live, to have a similarly good, firm, chewy texture when cooked, the flavour of true European lobster was more meaty and subtle, and the Canadian one was more directly salty/sweet-tasting.

If you decide to buy a ready-cooked lobster, make sure that its tail is tightly curled. A limp-tailed lobster indicates that it was dead and possibly deteriorating before it was cooked. A crab should feel heavy for its size, with no sound of liquid sloshing around inside.

Cornish Crab Soup | serves 6

1 large cooked crab
100g (3½oz) long-grain rice
1 litre (1¾ pints) milk
25g (1oz) butter
sea salt and freshly ground black pepper
freshly grated nutmeg
1 litre (1¾ pints) chicken stock
1 teaspoon anchovy essence
150ml (¼ pint) single cream

Place the rice, milk and butter in a pan with salt, pepper and nutmeg to taste. Bring to the boil, then simmer until the rice is tender. Add the brown crabmeat, setting aside the white meat from the claws. Rub the mixture through a sieve, or blend it in a liquidizer. Return it to the pan, add the chicken stock, anchovy essence and white crabmeat.

Adjust the seasoning, and stir in the cream. Heat the soup through without boiling.

Crab and Courgette Flan | serves 4

225g (8oz) shortcrust pastry
225g (8oz) courgettes
3 free-range eggs
300ml (½ pint) full-cream milk
2 tablespoons peeled and seeded diced tomato
sea salt and freshly ground black pepper
225g (8oz) fresh white crabmeat
fresh basil leaves

Roll the pastry out and line a 25cm (10 in) flan dish. Prick the base, line with greaseproof paper, fill with baking beans, and bake blind for 8 minutes in a preheated oven at 190°C/375°F/Gas 5. Meanwhile, slice the courgettes quite thin and blanch them briefly in boiling water. Drain, dry and cool them.

When the pastry case is cool, lay the courgette slices in the bottom. Beat the eggs into the milk, and stir in the diced tomato, together with a pinch of salt and pepper. Arrange the crabmeat on top of the courgettes, and pour on the egg mixture. Bake for 20–25 minutes with the oven at the same temperature, or slightly lower if the surface begins to brown too much. Serve warm. Garnish with torn-up basil leaves.

Crab Cakes | serves 6–8

85g (3oz) fresh breadcrumbs
2 tablespoons walnut or olive oil
2–3 tablespoons full-cream milk
1 teaspoon English mustard
½ teaspoon mild paprika
½ teaspoon Worcestershire sauce
¼ teaspoon Tabasco sauce
dash of Angostura bitters
juice of ½ lemon
1 teaspoon freshly ground black pepper
2 tablespoons freshly grated horseradish
450g (1lb) fresh white crabmeat
2 free-range eggs, separated
butter or oil for frying

For the garnish
lime or lemon wedges
fresh coriander

Soak the breadcrumbs in the oil and milk. Mix together the rest of the seasoning ingredients, including the horseradish, then stir in the crabmeat, the soaked breadcrumbs and the beaten egg yolks. Mix thoroughly. Whisk the egg whites to firm peaks, and fold into the crab mixture. Form into small cakes, and fry in oil or butter until golden-brown. Serve with lime or lemon wedges, and garnish with fresh coriander. A homemade tomato sauce makes a nice accompaniment, as does a horse-radish cream.

Double Lamb Cutlets with Crab, Lemon and Thyme Stuffing | serves 6

Shellfish and meat was a popular combination during the era of nouvelle cuisine, as it still is in American grill restaurants as 'surf 'n' turf'. It has long been a traditional combination in eastern France with such dishes as the crayfish-based Sauce Nantua, served with chicken. Similar recipes have long existed in the English/Welsh repertoire. Lamb or mutton was most often used; a crab stuffing for a leg of mutton or lamb, or roast lamb stuffed with cockles where some of the cockles were sliced and inserted into the outer flesh of the leg, as we might insert slivers of garlic.

Use the stuffing in this recipe for a boned leg or shoulder of lamb, or with lamb chops as well as with cutlets. This is a very easy recipe to scale down for 2 servings, if that suits you better.

6 double lamb cutlets, 4–5cm (1½–2in) thick
melted butter for brushing

For the stuffing
4 tablespoons fresh white breadcrumbs
6 tablespoons white crabmeat, together with any juices
grated zest of 1 lemon
a little lemon juice
2 teaspoons fresh thyme or lemon thyme leaves
¼ teaspoon ground mace

¼ teaspoon ground cardamom
sea salt and freshly ground black pepper
55g (2oz) butter, softened
1 free-range egg yolk

With a sharp knife, make a horizontal pocket in the lean eye of each lamb cutlet. Trim them of most of the fat.

Mix all the stuffing ingredients together. Divide the stuffing equally between the prepared cutlets. Or if you wish, remove the fillet from the bone altogether, making a noisette of lamb. Fill with the crab stuffing, and secure closed with wooden cocktail sticks, or tie into a neat parcel.

Grill for 15–20 minutes, or place on a rack in a roasting tin and roast in a preheated oven at 220°C/450°F/Gas 7 for 12–15 minutes, turning down a notch after 5 minutes. Baste with a little melted butter once or twice.

Lobster Stew | serves 1–2

When I was in Maine one summer, I learned a great deal about cooking lobsters, all of which can be applied to the fine lobsters landed in the small fishing ports which dot the West Country's coastline. The secret to a lobster stew is the maturing process. Unlike most shellfish dishes, this is best made well in advance. Whilst 2 days is said to improve it hugely, you can eat the stew within 6–7 hours. It must, of course, be cooled quickly, refrigerated and thoroughly reheated before serving.

1 small lobster, lightly and freshly cooked and still warm
55g (2oz) butter
300ml (½ pint) full-cream milk
sea salt and freshly ground black pepper

Take the coral and tomally (the soft, pale-green creamy flesh), and gently cook this in the butter in a heavy saucepan for 5–10 minutes, breaking up the coral with the back of the spoon. Cut the lobster tail meat into large chunks, and add this to the pan to cook for a further 10 minutes. Remove from the heat, season lightly, and allow to cool for 15–20 minutes. Scald the milk, then add gradually to the lobster, stirring continuously and no more than a trickle at a time. During the stirring, the stew should turn a delicate, pale salmon colour. When all the milk has been added, cool the stew, cover, and then refrigerate until required.

Crab or Lobster Bap

My very favourite way to eat crab and lobster is in a soft fresh roll. It is so simple to make that it needs no recipe. All you do is combine freshly cooked crab or lobster tail meat with good-quality mayonnaise, and generously fill a split, soft, buttered bap with it. This makes a perfect lunch with a glass of dry white wine, a good cider or cold beer on a hot day.

Meat, Poultry and Game

[illegible] winter [illegible] which [illegible]
only a penny [illegible] a good deal [illegible] husband [illegible]
difference between [illegible] and [illegible]
[illegible]

[illegible] the [illegible]
[illegible] present [illegible] West Country [illegible],
and [illegible] formed the [illegible] this
[illegible] I have [illegible] curiosity about [illegible]
get [illegible] table. I [illegible] the programme [illegible]
[illegible] producers [illegible] of my cooking in an
old [illegible] water-mill in [illegible] rural Cornwall.
[illegible] we were filming [illegible] in the West Country
[illegible]

[illegible]
[illegible]. But I do seem to [illegible] less of [illegible] these [illegible] is
not [illegible] tradition; the [illegible] is produced [illegible] high
welfare systems, with no [illegible] and reared [illegible]
rather [illegible] intensively [illegible], and having [illegible] a
premium for it. I expect to [illegible] often.

A few years ago, I wrote a book about meat, which covered not only cookery but a good deal about animal husbandry and the differences between factory farming and sustainable, humane forms of livestock rearing. Proposals for a television series on the subject fell on deaf ears at the time, and I put to one side my research material, gathered during countless visits to farms all over the country.

Then, at the end of 1994, I was delighted to be asked to write and present a cookery series for Westcountry Television, and then another one, both of which formed the basis of this book. Because I have an insatiable curiosity about how food gets to our table, I planned the programmes around ingredients and producers, with a final element of me cooking in an old converted water-mill in deepest, rural Cornwall.

Because we were filming in early spring in the West Country, I spent much time with livestock farmers. The herb gardens and cider orchards, the bee-keepers and the soft-fruit growers would have to wait for another season, for the West Country in spring has but one glorious crop – grass.

I like meat, to the extent that I am unlikely to become a vegetarian. But I do seem to eat less of it these days. This is not a contradiction; the meat I eat is produced under high welfare systems, with no feed additives and reared extensively rather than intensively, often organically, and, having to pay a premium for it, I expect to eat it less often.

I went to visit farmers all over Dorset, Devon, Somerset and Cornwall. Charlotte Russell looks after a herd of North and South Devon cows, at their most picturesque grazing on the high cliffs above Polruan, on the National Trust Churchtown Farm at Lantiglos, that she and her husband Mark are gradually converting to fully organic, when they will hope to sell their meat through local organic farm shops.

Anne Petch farms in the gentler countryside of North Devon, although it was a wild and windy day when I went to Heal Farm to visit her and her herd of English rare-breed pigs, which, as pork, ham and other products, are sent by mail order to customers all over the country. I did wonder if it wasn't a strange thing to do, to eat the meat from rare breeds. If they are rare, should we be eating them? But Anne assured me that only by creating a market for the meat will more people be encouraged to keep these native breeds, rather than just the skinny, modern, commercial pig. And these native breeds are so handsome and full of character – the dandyish russet Tamworth, the picture-book Gloucester Old Spot, the Middle White with its appealing squashed-looking face, not to mention the Berkshire, the Large Black, the Lop with its long floppy ears, and the Saddleback.

Henrietta Grieg, near Exeter, rears lambs, and Wensleydale sheep for mutton, on the hillside far above the noisy M5 motorway, with three generations of border collies: Tess, her mother and grandmother. Henrietta's husband, Peter, looks after the butchery, as well as sales and marketing, both for their shop in Exeter and the shop at Piper's Farm. Their lamb, which Peter butchers according to continental seaming techniques, following the line of the muscles rather than cutting into joints on the bone, is excellent – juicy, full of flavour and with a good texture – but it was the mutton I was most tempted by. It is very good to see something of a come-back in this traditional British meat. I commend my cobbler recipe (see page 134), which also uses a local cheese, Devon Garland, made by Jeremy Frankpitt.

I have known Bill Reynolds of Swaddles Green Farm for some years, after meeting him one day in Hampstead, where he was delivering organic meat to private customers from his refrigerated van. His London customer-base has expanded so much that he now drives up from his farm near the Blackdown Hills in Somerset to deliver on Thursdays and Fridays. His wife, Charlotte, looks after the poultry. Their chickens are excellent, but their ducks, free-range, organically reared birds, which followed us up and down the fields, are the best-tasting ducks I have ever eaten, so good that I do not think I shall be able to eat a supermarket duck again. A plain roasting suits the bird best, but I have also included a recipe for duck breasts using other local ingredients, a dish which I put on the menu at the Café Royal Grill Room when I cooked two West Country dinners there in autumn 1995.

The farmers I visited are all very clear about why they farm in this way, not least because of a concern for what their own children eat. They know that their animals have not been pumped full of growth promoters, nor have they been administered anything other than therapeutic drugs. And, too, they are interested in food and the quality of what they, and we, eat.

The recipes I cooked in the series are a mixture of slow dishes cooked in the Aga, which need only a little preparation time, after which they look after themselves, and dishes cooked quickly on the hob. When I came home from a long day out on location, however, something simple was the order of the day, and we ate bangers and mash more than once – Heal Farm and Swaddles Green Farm both produce majestic sausages. And my husband, Tom, cooked for me a few times, which impressed the crew greatly as they delivered me back home to these glorious smells wafting from the kitchen.

Mutton and Lamb

When I travel through the West Country by train, or by car, the first thing I notice is one of the most striking features of the landscape, and it really tells me where I am – sloping, lush green meadows on the steep hillsides, full of grazing sheep, and in the springtime, young lambs. Sheep have been domesticated since the earliest time, before even cattle and pigs, because they are easier to manage. They have been highly prized by farmers because of their strong herd instincts and are economical to feed as they eat grass rather than expensive cereals. Sheep can be kept where the land is unsuitable for cultivation of other crops.

In nineteenth-century England we liked to cook mutton or lamb with a little ginger or nutmeg, cloves or mace for seasoning. This preparation almost certainly had its origins in medieval cookery. There is a fifteenth-century recipe, for example, for breast of mutton, flavoured with cinnamon and saffron, and stewed in ale.

In Cornwall, lamb pie, cooked with plenty of onion and parsley, was finished off after baking by lifting up the crust, spreading on a layer of clotted cream, and replacing the lid.

Mutton Cobbler with a Devon Garland Topping | serves 6–8

Although I would not recommend mixing orange juice and red wine as a drink, the flavours work well together in this recipe for mutton.

Instead of the usual pie-crust, I have devised a topping of scone dough, flavoured with Devon Garland cheese, which, in turn, is flavoured with herbs and onions. You can prepare the meat 2–3 days in advance, and refrigerate until ready to cook. The topping will only take a few minutes to mix and roll out, and about 15 minutes to bake.

1.5kg (generous 3lb) diced mutton
1 tablespoon plain flour
½ teaspoon each sea salt and freshly ground black pepper
3 tablespoons olive oil
zest and juice of 1 orange
600ml (1 pint) good dry red wine
1 sprig of fresh rosemary

For the cheese topping
280g (10oz) self-raising flour
85g (3oz) butter or lard, diced
85g (3oz) Devon Garland or other West Country cheese, coarsely grated or finely diced
freshly ground black pepper

2 tablespoons plain yoghurt, mixed with 5 tablespoons cold water

Toss the mutton, a few pieces at a time, in a bag with the flour, salt and pepper. Brown the meat in the oil in a flameproof casserole, and then add the orange zest, juice and wine.

Bring to the boil, tuck in the sprig of rosemary, cover, and cook at 150°C/300°F/Gas 2 for about 3 hours, or cook it overnight or all day in the bottom oven of an Aga.

To make the cheese topping, rub the flour and fat together in a bowl, then stir in the cheese and pepper. Stir in enough yoghurt liquid to make a soft, pliable dough. Transfer to a floured board and knead lightly.

Roll out to fit the top of whatever ovenproof dish you are serving the cobbler from. Using the lid as a template, cut into wedges and lay them on top of the mutton stew. Bake in a preheated oven at 200°C/400°F/Gas 6 for 15–20 minutes.

Rack of Lamb with Three Mustards | serves 2

Not many roasts are suitable for only two people, but best end of lamb is ideal, with 6–7 small cutlets.

1 best end of lamb, chine bone removed
2 garlic cloves
1 tablespoon strong English mustard
1 tablespoon tarragon or other mild mustard
1 tablespoon English grain mustard
1 tablespoon chopped fresh tarragon
sea salt and freshly ground black pepper
juice of ½ lemon
1 tablespoon olive oil
25g (1oz) fine fresh breadcrumbs

If your butcher has not already done so, trim the lamb ribs right down to the thick, meaty flesh, and remove the outer layer of fat. When carved, this will give an 'eye' of meat on each well-trimmed bone, and thus very little fat. With the exception of the breadcrumbs, mix the rest of the ingredients and spread all over the surface of the meat. You can leave it to marinate overnight, or cook it immediately, as you prefer.

Make sure the meat is at room temperature when you cook it, which you should do in a preheated oven at 200°C/400°F/Gas 6 for 20 minutes, altogether. After 10 minutes, sprinkle the meat with breadcrumbs, and press them in lightly. Return the meat to the oven. When done, allow it to rest in a warm place for 15 minutes before carving. This will allow the juices to redistribute through the meat.

Lamb Shanks with Leeks and Barley | serves 4

1 large onion, peeled and sliced or chopped
1 tablespoon olive oil or sunflower oil
2–3 garlic cloves, peeled and crushed (optional)
4 lamb shanks
300ml (½ pint) red or white wine, lamb stock or water
1 teaspoon black peppercorns
sea salt
2 bay leaves
1–2 sprigs of fresh thyme
175g (6oz) pearl barley
450g (1lb) leeks

Fry the onion in the oil in a flameproof casserole until golden-brown, and add the garlic, if using it. Brown the lamb shanks all over, then add the wine, peppercorns, a little salt, bay leaves, thyme and barley. Bring to the boil, cover and simmer for 1 hour.

Meanwhile, trim, slice and wash the leeks. If you are using baby leeks, leave them whole. After the lamb has been cooking for an hour, add the leeks, stir to cover them with the juices, then continue cooking until the lamb, barley and leeks are tender.

Note

The casserole can also be cooked in a preheated oven at 180°C/350°F/Gas 4, for about 2 hours, or for longer at a lower temperature if more convenient.

Poached Leg of Lamb | serves 6,plus leftovers

2kg (about 4lb) whole leg of lamb
2 bay leaves
1 onion, peeled and stuck with 6 cloves
parsley stalks
1 carrot, peeled and sliced
1 small turnip, peeled and sliced
1 leek, washed and sliced
1 celery stalk, trimmed and sliced
sea salt and freshly ground black pepper

Trim and tie the leg of lamb to hold its shape. Fill a large saucepan or fish kettle with enough water to cover the lamb. Test it first. Put in all the ingredients apart from the lamb. Bring to the boil, add the lamb, and when the water comes back to the boil, turn down the heat as low as possible, and poach for 15 minutes per 450g (1lb).

Remove the lamb from the pot, and put it to rest in a warm place for about 15 minutes before carving.

Goat and Kid

In Hardy's Wessex, Audrey and Harry Fuller rear Boer goats near Sherborne, where Sir Walter Raleigh had the freehold of the castle given to him by Elizabeth I. Apparently the sixteenth-century courtier gave up trying to convert the twelfth-century fortress into a desirable residence, and built himself a new castle instead. Times do not always change as much as we think.

The meat from the Fullers' goats and kids is sold through Barrow Boar, at South Barrow between Glastonbury Tor and Cadbury Castle, the ley lines flowing right through the middle of the farm. At Barrow Boar you can buy all manner of unusual meats, including imported ostrich, alligator and kangaroo, as well as native peacocks, and the wild boar bred by Nigel Dauncy. But it was the kid meat that I was particularly keen to cook. I'd often eaten kid in southern Europe, and occasionally I've cooked it at home. It is a really excellent meat, lean, full of flavour, quite tender, and altogether a suitable dish for the Sunday lunch table. And leftovers make excellent sandwiches, as the crew discovered at lunch the day after the kitchen shoot.

Leg of Kid 'Boulangère' | serves 4

If you can get it, try replacing the rosemary with lavender. It is excellent with both kid and lamb, and will not overperfume your meat, just give it a subtle fragrant hint.

1 leg of kid, weighing about 1.5kg (generous 3lb)
4 tablespoons olive oil
1 head of fresh large-clove garlic
3–4 potatoes, peeled and thinly sliced
2 large onions, peeled and thinly sliced
1 sprig of fresh thyme or rosemary
a few fresh parsley sprigs
sea salt and freshly ground black pepper
glass of dry white or red wine

For the garnish
chopped fresh parsley

Brown the joint all over in 1–2 tablespoons of the oil. Leave the garlic cloves whole, but separate and peel them and cut into thin slivers. Insert these under the thin layer of fat and skin at intervals.

Preheat the oven to 180°C/350°F/Gas4. Put half the potatoes and onions in the bottom of a well-soaked Romertopf, a lidded unglazed earthenware pot, a chicken brick or roasting tin. Lay the meat on top, and cover with the rest of the onions.

Add the herbs, season lightly, and pour on the wine and the rest of the oil. Put on the lid, and cook for 2–2¼ hours, until the meat is tender.

Serve sprinkled with parsley.

Shepherd's Pie | serves 4–6

With leftover mutton, lamb or kid, make this classic 'Monday' dish, inexpensive and easy to prepare. These potato-topped pies can be made from scratch, using raw lamb mince, but they are ideal for using up the remains of a large joint.

Grated cheese, egg yolks, herbs, cream and spring onions are just some of the ingredients which can be added to the mashed potato to dress it up if you think it needs it. Incidentally, cottage pie is the version using leftover minced beef.

1 medium onion, peeled and finely chopped
1 tablespoon olive oil
675g (1½lb) cooked lamb or kid, minced, or finely chopped
200ml (7fl oz) lamb stock or gravy
2 tablespoons port
1 teaspoon Worcestershire sauce
pinch of freshly grated nutmeg
pinch of ground allspice
pinch of chopped fresh rosemary
1 tablespoon finely chopped fresh parsley
sea salt and freshly ground black pepper
900g (2lb) mashed potatoes

Lightly brown the onion in the oil. Mix with the rest of the ingredients, except for the potatoes, and spoon into an ovenproof dish. Spread the mashed potatoes over the top, and score with the tines of a fork.

Bake in the top of a preheated oven at 180°C/350°F/Gas 4 for about 45 minutes.

Pork

It is curious that, while whole sucking pigs and boar's head have played their role in festive eating in many cultures and over many centuries, pork has never been part of haute cuisine. It has remained a homely, peasant food, and indeed, one pig provided the main supply of meat for peasant families in the past, as it does today. It was known as 'the gentleman that pays the rent'; no part of the pig was wasted.

Braised Hand of Pork with Rice and Oriental Flavours | serves 6

For this recipe, it is important to choose a piece of pork, on the bone, with plenty of skin and a good deal of fat. The skin should be left on, but it can be scored. I have made this with belly pork, knuckle, shoulder and top leg, and find that the hand of pork, part of the shoulder, has just the right proportion of meat, skin and bone. The dried mushrooms, tangerine peel and spices are available from oriental grocers.

about 1.5kg (3lb) hand of pork with the trotter
2 tablespoons soy sauce
1 tablespoon rice vinegar or sherry vinegar
1 tablespoon toasted sesame oil
2 teaspoons Szechuan peppercorns, crushed
1 teaspoon five-spice powder
1–2 teaspoons molasses or dark muscovado sugar
2 star anise pods
4 cloves
1–2 onions, peeled and sliced
1 piece of tangerine peel, soaked and shredded
8 dried Chinese mushrooms, soaked and sliced
1.25 litres (2 pints) water or stock
450g (1lb) Jasmine or Thai fragrant rice
fresh coriander leaves, chopped
3–4 spring onions, chopped

Rub the pork all over with the soy sauce, vinegar, sesame oil, pepper, five-spice powder and molasses or sugar. Leave overnight, or for a few hours. Put it into a deep flameproof casserole with the star anise, cloves, onions, tangerine peel and mushrooms, and any remaining marinade, together with 5–6 tablespoons water or stock.

Cover the casserole with a lid, and cook in the lower half of a preheated oven at 150°C/300°F/Gas 2 for about 2 hours. Remove the lid and add the rice, remaining water or stock, coriander and spring onions.

Stir well, bring to the boil on top of the stove, and put back in the oven for a further 45–60 minutes. Add more liquid if necessary, but the dish should be quite moist and sticky. Serve from the casserole.

Note

This eats well with chopsticks, the meat falling away from the bone. Soy sauce, toasted sesame oil and a little chilli/vinegar sauce can also be served separately, and fresh coriander leaves added just before serving, for both flavour and decorative effect.

Pork Pie with Traditional Hot-water Crust Pastry | gives 10 × 2cm (¾in) slices

If we are not careful, the real pork pie will be on its way to extinction. What is available commercially is one of the most degenerated of all food products, full of additives, cereal and scraps of meat and gristle.

A homemade pork pie is a beautiful sight, tall and proud, with crisp, firm golden pastry, glazed on the top, encasing succulent, tender meat in a flavoursome jelly.

For the stock
1 pig's trotter, split in two
1kg (2lb) pork bones
2 litres (3½–4 pints) water
1 carrot
1 celery stalk
12 black peppercorns

For the filling
500g (generous 1lb fat belly of pork)
115g (4oz) streaky bacon
500g (generous 1lb) lean pork meat, off the bone
1 teaspoon freshly ground black pepper
¼ teaspoon freshly grated nutmeg
1 tablespoon finely chopped fresh parsley
½ tablespoon finely chopped fresh sage or thyme

For the hot-water pastry
up to 675g (1½lb) plain flour
1 tablespoon sea salt
250g (9oz) lard
200ml (7fl oz) water

Make the stock. Simmer all the ingredients together for 3–4 hours, strain and reduce to 600ml (1 pint).

Remove the rind from the belly of pork and bacon (the rind can be added to the stock pot), and mince the two together. Fry quickly in batches, if necessary, just enough to remove the raw look. Dice the lean pork, and fry it in the same way, draining off any cooking liquid into the stock. Mix the meats together, and add the spices and herbs. Cover, and stand in a cool place.

Make the pastry, either in a bowl or on a marble slab, or, as I make it, in a food processor. Sift together the flour and salt, keeping back about 5 tablespoons of flour. Put the lard and water into a saucepan, bring to the boil, stirring continuously, and slowly add the flour. When the dry and liquid ingredients are thoroughly blended together in a hot, smooth (rather than sticky) mass, turn on to a work top and knead, adding more flour, as necessary, to form a workable dough.

Cut off a quarter of the pastry to use as a lid, and press or roll out the rest to line a 1kg (2lb) loaf tin, leaving about 1cm (½in) of pastry hanging over the rim of the tin. Fill with the pork filling mixture, slightly moulding it in the centre.

Roll out the remaining pastry, and use to cover the pie. Press the edges together, roll them over once inside the rim of the loaf tin (that way, it will be an easy matter to slide a palette knife all the way round the pie when cold to ease it out of the tin), and make a fluted edge by pinching together at intervals.

Roll out the pastry trimmings to make stick-on decorations, if you wish. Make a pencil-diameter hole in the top of the pastry, and keep it open with a small roll of greaseproof paper. Brush the pie with milk, or egg, to glaze it, and lay two or three layers of greaseproof paper or kitchen foil on top so that the crust does not bake too brown.

Bake in the centre of a preheated oven at 170°C/325°F/Gas3 for 1¼ hours. Remove the paper for the last 15 minutes. Let the pie cool for 2–3 hours, then slowly pour in, through the hole in the pastry, as much of the pint of reduced stock as you can. Allow to cool completely. Then wrap in foil, or greaseproof paper, to store. Do not keep the pie for more than 2–3 days in the refrigerator before eating it.

Mint, Honey and Cider-glazed Pork Chops

serves 4

Mint is usually associated with lamb, but I dislike our traditional mint sauce. Instead, I look back to the uses of the herb in Roman cookery and find that this combination of mint with honey, cider and spices is a delightful one, that surprisingly also goes very well with fish.

Lentils or mashed potatoes are a good accompaniment, as is a purée of onions or leeks, or a heap of sauerkraut. If vegetables do not appeal, serve instead either a green salad or a chunky salad of fennel, apple, walnuts and white radish.

4 thick pork chops
5–6 sprigs of fresh mint
½ teaspoon sea salt
freshly ground black pepper
1 teaspoon ground cumin
1 teaspoon ground coriander
3 tablespoons cider
1 tablespoon cider vinegar
1 tablespoon clear honey
1 teaspoon mustard

Trim the pork chops, and snip the fat so that it does not curl.

Strip the leaves from the mint, and roughly tear them. Put into a mortar with the salt, pepper and spices, and grind to a paste with a pestle. Gradually add the cider, vinegar, honey and mustard.

Brush this paste on the chops, and leave for 20–30 minutes for the flavours to penetrate the meat.

Heat the grill, and put the chops under it. Turn down the heat after 4–5 minutes, and continue cooking for 4–5 minutes more. Raise the heat, turn over the meat, and finish the cooking, turning down the heat once more after a few minutes.

Serve hot with your chosen accompaniment.

Jellied Ham with Parsley | serves 4–6

1 ham hock, about 675–900g (1½–2lb)
300ml (½ pint) good dry white wine
1 onion, peeled
3 cloves
1 bay leaf
6 parsley stalks
6 black peppercorns
3–4 tablespoons finely chopped fresh parsley
sea salt and freshly ground black pepper

Soak the ham in cold water for at least 4 hours, changing the water a few times. If the ham was not too salty to begin with, you can always add salt later, if necessary.

Put the ham into a saucepan with the wine, onion, cloves, bay leaf, parsley stalks and peppercorns. Cover with water, bring to the boil, skim the surface, and simmer, partly covered, for 1½–2 hours, until the meat is tender. Remove the joint from the pan, keeping the stock simmering.

When cool enough to handle, remove the meat from the bone, and put the bone and skin, but not the fat, back into the pan to extract more gelatine. Remove any sinews from the meat, and dice it neatly. Wet a mould or pudding basin, and put the meat into it loosely, not packing it down, as the liquid is meant to fill the spaces between the meat. Cover and refrigerate.

Strain the liquid into a chilled bowl. This is to bring the temperature down as quickly as possible so that you can chill the stock in the refrigerator in order to remove the fat from the surface. Once this has been done, liquefy the stock again. Stir in the parsley, and pour it over the meat, stirring to mix it well. Season to taste only at this point, then refrigerate, covered, until it sets again. Eat within 2 days.

Ham in Puff Pastry | serves 6

450g (1lb) puff pastry
175g (6oz) Menallack or Farmhouse Cheddar cheese, grated
300ml (½ pint) thick béchamel
350g (12oz) sliced ham
freshly grated nutmeg
free-range egg beaten with milk, to glaze

Roll out the pastry to about 5mm (¼ in) thick, and cut into two rectangles, one about 2.5–4cm (1–1½ in) larger than the other all the way round. Mix the grated cheese into the béchamel, and spread half of it over the larger rectangle, leaving a border of the dimensions described above. Lay on the slices of ham, overlapping, and spread the remaining béchamel on top. Dust with a little nutmeg, and cover with the second rectangle of pastry. Brush the border with egg glaze. Fold over on to the top layer of pastry, and press and pinch to seal. Make one or two slashes in the pastry to let the steam escape. Glaze and transfer to a baking sheet.

Bake in a preheated oven at 180°C/350°F/Gas 4 for 45–60 minutes.

In Praise of Sausages

Since my stay in the West Country, I have become increasingly enthusiastic about sausages, for it is clear that the real British banger has emerged at last from the heap of nastiness with a 'sausage' label attached to it foisted on us for so long. Some of the nastiness still exists in sausages so cheap that you wonder what they can possibly contain but would rather not know. As with most things, you get what you pay for; a cheap sausage will be a cheap sausage. It is worth paying top price for the best-quality sausage and making a meal of it, whether that meal is breakfast, lunch or supper.

In fact, there is no single British banger but many. Apart from the classic Cumberland and Lincolnshire sausages, butchers all over the country are making sausages to their own recipes, some new, some researched from old cookery books, many of them prizewinners. Specialist sausage-makers are extending the boundaries of the accepted view of the sausage all the time, so that herbs, spices, fruit and vegetables are combined with a variety of meats, not always successfully but with a good deal of imagination.

Toad-in-the-hole is a popular dish with expatriates and I often put it on my menus when I'm cooking in hotels abroad. The butcher chef at such hotels is usually Swiss or German, and before we get down to making up a batch of sausages, I have to put up with jokes about there not being enough bread in the bakery to make English sausages.

The secret to a successful 'toad', apart from excellent sausages, is to have the greased roasting tin very hot before you pour in the batter. The best way to ensure this is to cook the sausages in the roasting tin in a hot oven for about 10–15 minutes first, and then pour in the batter.

Bangers and Mash | serves 4–6

One of my favourite dishes, both for easy suppers and for entertaining, is bangers and mash.

Mash is usually simply mashed potatoes, but mashed potatoes are no longer simple. They come flavoured with olive oil, saffron, pesto, spices, garlic, herbs, chopped dried tomatoes, spring onions, chopped olives. Or they are combined with other root vegetables, and this is the approach I favour for bangers and mash.

After much experimenting, I find it is hard to beat plain mashed potatoes, although I also like a combination of potatoes and sweet potatoes with coarse sausages. With game sausages, however, I would make celeriac and potato mash, as I would for other game dishes.

675g (1½lb) sausages
675g (1½lb) large potatoes, peeled
450g (1lb) sweet potato, peeled
peeled cloves of 1 head of garlic
sea salt and freshly ground black pepper

Put the sausages into a lightly greased pan to prevent them sticking, and bake them in a preheated oven at 180°C/350°F/ Gas 4 for about 40 minutes, or for a shorter time in a hotter oven. The sausages can also be grilled, or fried, of course, but I like the even cooking and browning produced by the oven.

Meanwhile, cut the potatoes and sweet potato into even chunks and boil with the garlic. Drain, mash and season, and heap on to a serving dish. Arrange the sausages on top and serve.

Spicy Sausage Roll | makes 12–16 slices

This recipe makes a good, substantial accompaniment to a tasting of red wines, as an alternative to bread and cheese.

450g (1lb) sausages
4 tablespoons port, red vermouth or amontillado sherry
2 shallots or 1 small onion, peeled, finely chopped and lightly fried
1 tablespoon finely chopped fresh parsley, sage or watercress
1 teaspoon ground allspice
½ teaspoon crushed cardamom seeds
1 teaspoon fresh ground black pepper (optional)
350g (12oz) puff pastry
2–3 tablespoons Dijon or grain mustard
milk or beaten egg, to glaze (optional)

Slit open the sausages, and squeeze the meat into a bowl. Mix in the port, vermouth or sherry, the shallots, or onion, herbs and spices, and blend thoroughly. You may like to add some black pepper, but it is unlikely that you will need to add salt. Roll the pastry out to a rectangle measuring about 20 × 30cm (8 × 12in), and spread with the mustard. Spoon the sausage meat in a line along the length of the pastry, and brush the long edges with water. Carefully roll up, press the pastry edge to seal, and place the roll on a greased and floured baking sheet, with the join underneath. Slash with a knifepoint in 2–3 places on top to allow steam to escape, brush with milk or egg, if you wish, and bake in a preheated oven at 190°C/375°F/Gas 5 for 20–25 minutes. Allow to cool slightly before cutting into slices to serve.

Hotcakes | makes 6–7 large ones

If you have time to make them for breakfast, as they are a perfect accompaniment to sausages, bacon and eggs, here is my recipe for hotcakes: very easy and very versatile.

1 free-range egg
150ml (¼ pint) semi-skimmed or skimmed milk
1 heaped tablespoon plain yoghurt
115g (4oz) plain flour
1 teaspoon baking powder
oil or butter for frying

Beat the egg, milk, yoghurt and flour to a thick, smooth, lump-free batter. Beat in the baking powder, and wait until it begins to froth and bubble slightly on the surface. This indicates that the mixture is aerating because of the baking powder's action and will produce a light batter.

Make sure the frying pan and fat are hot (or use a non-stick pan). Pour in the batter until it covers the area of a small saucer. Do not shake the pan or spread the mixture. When the surface of the hotcake is matt, dry and full of holes, turn it over, and cook the underside for 2–3 minutes. Stack the hotcakes on a plate, set over a pan of hot water, until you have cooked all the batter.

Wild Boar and Game

A few hundred years ago, herds, or sounds, of wild boar roaming English heaths and moorland would have been a common sight. But woe betide anyone other than landed gentry who caught and killed one of these magnificent beasts.

The wild boar being reared in Britain now are related to Polish, German or other European strains, the English breed having died out. The meat is increasingly available, both by mail order and in a few specialist shops and supermarkets. A leg of wild boar makes a marvellous alternative to the Christmas turkey or other festive dish.

Roast Haunch of Wild Boar with Gin, Blackcurrant Liqueur, Coriander and Juniper, on a Bed of Celeriac | serves 8–10,plus leftovers

For this recipe which I cooked in the series I used an animal from Robin Hanbury-Tenison's magnificent herd of wild boar that roam over a large, albeit securely enclosed, part of Bodmin Moor, amongst the gorse thickets. Mark Menhinick, the butcher in Wadebridge, did an excellent job of dressing the carcase, and together we chose the leg, agreeing that it would produce an extremely tasty joint, which indeed it did.

The recipe I developed also uses other West Country ingredients, including Plymouth gin, Devon blackcurrant liqueur and grain mustard.

1 haunch (leg) of wild boar
1 tablespoon juniper berries
1 tablespoon coriander seeds
leaves of a good sprig of fresh rosemary, snipped
1 tablespoon coarse sea salt
2 tablespoons English grain mustard
grated zest of 2 lemons,
juice of 1 lemon
1 tablespoon freshly ground black pepper
150ml (¼ pint) Plymouth gin
4–5 tablespoons Devon blackcurrant liqueur
1–1.5kg (generous 2–3lb) prepared celeriac

Have the boar skin removed in one piece. Trim off much of the fat and wipe the meat all over.

Grind the juniper berries, coriander seeds and rosemary with the salt, and mix with the rest of the ingredients other than the celeriac. Rub the paste over the meat, cover with the skin, and leave for an hour or two, or overnight if more convenient.

Peel and trim the celeriac into cork-sized pieces and arrange in a greased roasting dish. Place the haunch on top, cover with the skin, and cook in a preheated oven at 150°C/ 300°F/ Gas2 for 25–30 minutes per 450g (1lb), plus, at the end, a further 20 minutes at 200°C/400°F/Gas6. Allow the meat to rest for 20 minutes before discarding the skin and carving the meat into thin slices.

Serve with extra root vegetables, roasted in the oven, steamed vegetables such as celery, leeks and fennel, and the celeriac made into a purée. Make a gravy with the boiled-down meat juices, and serve with a little homemade sharp fruit jelly (see page 307) as an accompaniment.

Wild Boar and Grouse Pie

This game pie was another of the recipes I put on the menu at the Café Royal Grill Room in London when I cooked some West Country dinners there. It is moist and full of flavour. I generally marinate the meat for 24 hours, and bake the pie at least 24 hours before I need it. Unbroached, it will keep for up to a week in the refrigerator.

The pie will serve about 30 people if you have a large enough mould, otherwise use 2–3 moulds, ideally ones that will unclip to release the pie.

3 grouse
500g (generous 1lb) wild boar loin, cut into strips
600ml (1 pint) good red wine
150ml (¼ pint) extra virgin olive oil
2–3 garlic cloves, peeled and crushed (optional)
sea salt and freshly ground black pepper
1 sprig of fresh rosemary
12 juniper berries
1 tablespoon green peppercorns
1 tablespoon pink peppercorns
1.5kg (generous 3lb) shortcrust pastry
1kg (generous 2lb) wild boar meat, breast or shoulder, including the fat
450g (1lb) chicken livers
1.5kg (generous 3lb) belly pork, minced

150ml (¼ pint) amontillado sherry
1 free-range egg, plus 1 extra egg yolk beaten with milk, to glaze

Cut the breasts off the grouse, cut into 3–4 strips and marinate with the wild boar loin in the wine, and oil with the garlic, seasoning, herbs and spices for several hours or overnight. Meanwhile, make a game stock with the rest of the grouse (and some other game and meat bones). Remove the meat and reserve the herbs and spices from the marinade.

Roll out the pastry to about 1cm (½in) thick, and line a tin mould with three-quarters of it, being careful to avoid breaks in the pastry. Mince the wild boar breast or shoulder with the chicken livers, pork and seasonings from the marinade, and add the sherry and 1 egg; mix thoroughly again. Spoon a third of the mixture into the mould, and flatten with the back of a spoon. Lay a row of marinated strips on top, alternating boar with grouse. Repeat this, finishing with a layer of forcemeat. Pour a little of the game stock into the pie. Cover the top of the pie with the remaining pastry and seal the edges. Make a hole for the steam, and after decorating with pastry trimmings, paint with egg and milk glaze.

Bake in a preheated oven at 220°C/425°F/Gas 7 for 45 minutes, then for a further 45 minutes at 180°C/350°F/Gas 4.

Leave to cool in the mould, adding more rich stock if the pie will take it, and refrigerate until required. Cut in slices, and serve with spiced pears or other fruit preserve, jelly or chutney. Bring the sliced pie to room temperature before serving.

Peppered Country Casserole | serves 6,plus leftovers

This recipe is an immensely versatile dish, using a mixture of pigeon, venison and hare, although other combinations of meat and game can be used. I like to add plenty of spices and pepper to the casserole, but no single one dominates, simply adds to the layers of flavour.

1.5kg (generous 3lb) hare, venison and pigeon, off the bone
2 onions, peeled and chopped or sliced
2 tablespoons olive oil
1 pinch each ground mace, cinnamon, ginger and cumin
grating of nutmeg
1 teaspoon freshly ground black pepper
5g (1/6oz) square of bitter chocolate
600ml (1 pint) good dry red wine
300ml (½ pint) game or other meat stock
2 bay leaves
1 sprig of fresh thyme

For the garnish
watercress sprigs

Make sure the meat is cut into roughly even-sized pieces. Dry them thoroughly. Brown the onions in the oil, and transfer to a flameproof casserole. Brown the meat in batches, and transfer also to the casserole. Add the spices, pepper, chocolate and half the wine to the browning pan. Bring to the boil, scrape up any residues stuck to the pan, then add the remaining wine and stock. Bring to a full boil, pour over the meat, tuck in the herbs, cover, and cook in a preheated oven at 150°C/300°F/Gas2 for about 2 hours, or until the meat is tender. Serve from an earthenware dish, garnished with a sprig or two of watercress.

Note

Serve the casserole with jacket potatoes, put into the oven at the same time, or dauphinois potatoes. Root vegetables or green vegetables will accompany it very well too.

The casserole can be made and served immediately, or it can be cooked 2–3 days before required and refrigerated. It reheats well. Sometimes I serve the casserole with a crumble, sometimes with a herb cobbler topping, and sometimes with a crust of flaky pastry. Leftovers, chopped up and mixed with plenty of gravy, make a fine sauce for chunky pasta. Without the gravy, it makes good potted game, mixed with softened butter, spices and a little port or Madeira.

Beef

The beef I bought in the West Country was some of the best I've ever tasted. Riverford Farm Shop, near Totnes in Devon, and, nearer to where we were living, Trudgian Farm Shop in Probus, both sold beef from the native Devon breeds of cattle. The dark, ruby-red North Devon and the brighter South Devon are large animals, with a configuration that does not necessarily lend itself to the polystyrene supermarket tray. A joint of Devon beef is huge and majestic, of the kind that made British beef justly famous. Despite all that has happened in recent years in the British beef industry, I would have no hesitation about buying beef from these sources and from the farmers I met.

Their animals are bred and reared within closed beef herds, suckled at grass with their mothers and allowed to grow slowly and naturally on grass. Some are not slaughtered until over three years, the time it takes for them to reach their natural finished weight. This produces a mature and extremely flavourful meat, which is only enhanced by careful butchering and hanging.

The virtues of wing rib joint and fillet steak hardly need extolling, and so I decided to concentrate on some of the less well-known cuts of beef, such as shoulder and shin, as well as oxtail. These are inexpensive cuts, because they are less tender and require slower cooking, but every bit as good to eat as the prime cuts.

Exeter Stew | serves 6–8

1kg (generous 2lb) shoulder beef, off the bone
2 tablespoons cider vinegar
3 onions, peeled and sliced
25g (1oz) butter
25g (1oz) plain flour
850ml (1½ pints) cider, or ale
sea salt and freshly ground black pepper

For the dumplings
115g (4oz) plain flour
55g (2oz) suet, finely grated
1 tablespoon finely chopped fresh parsley
½ teaspoon chopped fresh thyme
½ teaspoon chopped fresh chives
½ teaspoon sea salt
½ teaspoon baking powder
grinding of black pepper

Trim the meat, and cut into a dozen or so pieces. Put into a casserole with the vinegar, and place in the bottom half of a preheated oven at 150°C/300°F/Gas2.

Gently fry the onions in the butter, sprinkle on the flour, and let it brown all over. Stir in the cider or ale, bring to the boil, and pour over the meat. Season lightly. Cover, return to the oven, and cook for 3 hours.

About 40 minutes before the end of cooking time, place dumplings on top of the meat. Make these by mixing all the ingredients together and shaping into small balls, adding a little milk, or water, if necessary.

To serve the stew, pile the meat into a serving dish with the sauce strained over it and the dumplings arranged around it. A good sprinkling of chopped flat-leaf parsley would also be very good.

Feather Steaks with Cider, Apple Juice and Black Pepper | serves 4

This is a quick stove-top recipe which makes the most of one of the lesser-known cuts of beef, feather steak. It is to the forequarter what fillet is to the hindquarter: tender, full of flavour and about a third of the price.

4 feather steaks, each weighing 115–150g (4–5oz)
1 tablespoon extra virgin olive oil or nut of butter
sea salt and freshly ground black pepper
6 tablespoons dry cider
3 tablespoons apple juice

Trim any fat from the meat. Heat the oil or butter in a heavy frying pan, and fry the meat on both sides until it is done to your liking.

Season, particularly with coarsely ground black pepper, and place on serving plates. Put the cider and apple juice into the pan, boil, scrape up any residues and spoon on to the steaks. Serve immediately.

Steak and Kidney Pie | serves 6–8

This English classic is a simple everyday dish that can be prepared in advance. Once the meat is cooking, it will look after itself and timing is not crucial.

The pastry can be homemade or bought, and the meat can be cooked and refrigerated overnight. All that remains to be done is to roll out the pastry, assemble, and bake the pie, which in all should take no more than 45 minutes.

900g (2lb) lean cut of beef, such as blade, chuck or topside
225g (8oz) trimmed lamb's kidney
25g (1oz) plain flour
½ teaspoon freshly ground black pepper
¼ teaspoon sea salt
pinch of ground mace
2 tablespoons sunflower or groundnut oil
1 onion, peeled and sliced
300ml (½ pint) beef stock
300ml (½ pint) brown ale or dry cider
1 bay leaf
280g (10oz) puff pastry
beaten free-range egg and milk, to glaze

Cut the beef and kidney into bite-size cubes, snipping away any fat from the interior of the kidney. Dry the kidney pieces. Put the flour and seasonings into a paper bag, and shake a few pieces of meat at a time in it to give them a light dusting of flour.

In a heavy pan or flameproof casserole, heat the oil, and fry the onion until golden. Push to one side, and brown the meat, a few pieces at a time. Pour on a little of the stock, and scrape up any residues stuck to the pan. Add the rest of the stock, the ale or cider, and the bay leaf. Bring to the boil, reduce the heat to a simmer, cover, and cook for about an hour until the beef is tender. Cool the meat quickly, and either cover and refrigerate until required, or transfer it to a pie dish.

Roll out the pastry, and use to cover the meat in the pie dish, pressing down well to seal at the edges. Lop off any excess pastry, and use it for trimming the pie. Slash the top to let the steam escape. Brush with the glaze. Bake in a preheated oven at 200°C/400°F/Gas6 for 30–35 minutes.

Note

I would suggest serving this with a purée of celeriac and a crisp, green vegetable, such as broccoli, or Savoy cabbage.

Potted Beef

This is a good way of using up leftovers from a joint of beef, delicious on toast or in sandwiches.

Using a food processor, put diced, cooked beef into the bowl with a pinch of mace, some freshly ground black pepper, softened butter in equal proportion to the meat, or less butter if you prefer, and a dash of port or Madeira. Blend until smooth, spoon into a bowl, and pour clarified butter over the top, which will seal it until required.

Leftover duck, turkey, venison and lamb can be dealt with in the same way.

Braised Beef in Red Wine | serves 6–8

900g–1.1kg (2–2½lb) blade of beef, in a piece
2 tablespoons plain flour
¼ teaspoon each ground mace, black pepper, cloves, cinnamon and cardamom
2 tablespoons olive oil
2 onions, peeled and thickly sliced
2 celery stalks, trimmed, and cut into 4 pieces
1 carrot and 1 leek, peeled and sliced
1 small turnip, peeled and diced
300ml (½ pint) good dry red wine
2–3 sprigs of fresh thyme
1 bay leaf

Trim the meat. Mix the flour and spices, and lightly coat the meat with it. Heat the oil in a flameproof casserole, and brown the meat all over. Remove and put to one side while you brown the vegetables all over. Put these to one side while you deglaze the casserole with half the wine, scraping up any residues. Flame the wine, and let it reduce for a few minutes more. Put back the vegetables and place the beef on top. Tuck in the herbs, cover, and cook very slowly on top of the stove, or in a preheated oven at 150°C/300°F/Gas 2, or even lower, for 2½–3 hours, which should give you a juicily tender piece of meat. Add a little wine from time to time, or if you are letting the meat cook in your absence, add half of it before you go out, and then, when ready to serve, boil up the rest of the wine with the cooking juices to make a good gravy. Slice the meat, and serve it with plenty of gravy and smooth mashed potatoes, or if cooking the meat in the oven, bake a few jacket potatoes. You can thicken the sauce by sieving some of the cooked vegetables into it.

Oxtail and Potato Tart | serves 4

Looking a little like a savoury *tarte tatin* when it is turned out, this is a handsome, impressive dish and well worth spending time on. In fact, the preparation is not difficult, and the oxtail is indeed better if cooked the day before required to allow you to degrease it. Oxtail is one of the cheapest cuts of meat, very versatile in soups and stews, and ideal for late autumn and winter, with its lip-sticking, homely quality.

1 oxtail, cut into 5cm (2 in) chunks
1 tablespoon olive oil
1 large onion, peeled and sliced
2 bay leaves
½ bottle good red wine
300ml (½ pint) water or beef stock
1.35kg (3 lb) large potatoes
6 prunes, pitted
85–115g (3–4oz) butter, salted or unsalted, as you prefer
sea salt and freshly ground black pepper

Brown the oxtail in the oil in a frying pan, and transfer the pieces to a casserole. Lightly brown the onion too, before transferring to the casserole. Tuck in the bay leaves.

Pour the wine into the frying pan, and bring to the boil, scraping up any caramelized cooking juices stuck to the bottom of the pan. Pour over the oxtail.

Add enough stock or water to come about three-quarters of the way to covering the meat. Simmer or cook in a very low oven for 2–3 hours, until the meat is tender.

Strain the cooking juices into a bowl. Cool, then refrigerate until next day, when you can lift off the layer of fat.

When the meat is cool enough to handle, remove all the bones, put the meat into a container, cover, and refrigerate until next day.

When ready to make the tart, peel and cut the potatoes into about 2mm (⅛ in) slices. Blanch them for 30 seconds or so in boiling water, then drain and rinse under cold running water. Lay the slices on a clean tea-towel to dry.

Chop the prunes, and mix them with the meat and a few spoonfuls of the by now jellied cooking juices.

Line with greaseproof paper and thickly butter a cake tin about 20–23 cm (8–9 in) diameter, and about 4 cm (1½ in) deep. Neatly arrange slices over the bottom of the tin, overlapping them to cover it completely – 2 layers will not be too much. Season lightly with salt and pepper. Take the longer slices of potato, and arrange these around the side of the tin, overhanging the top slightly.

Put the meat mixture into the lined tin, make it level, and fold over the potatoes at the edge. Cover with another neatly overlapping layer of potatoes. Season the top. Butter the surface, and cover loosely with a sheet of kitchen foil or greaseproof paper. Bake in a preheated oven at about 190°C/375°F/Gas 5 for about 45–50 minutes, until the potatoes are cooked through and nicely browned.

Before turning out on to a plate, weight the tart down for 15 minutes or so to firm it up and make cutting a little easier. With a sharp knife, cut into wedges and serve.

Note

I like to serve this with a purée of swede and garlic, lightly flavoured with clove or cardamom, or creamed cabbage flavoured with nutmeg. It is a marvellous winter dish.

Spiced Pressed Beef with Grouse

serves 10 as a starter, or use as a sandwich filling

900g (2lb) rump steak in a thick piece
breasts of 2 young grouse
freshly ground black pepper
6 juniper berries
6 cloves
6 allspice berries
large blade of mace
5–6 tablespoons port
5 tablespoons beef or game stock made from the trimmings of grouse carcases and beef
1 bay leaf
clarified butter

Slice the rump steak about 1cm (½in) thick. Remove the fillets from under the grouse breasts, and cut the breasts into strips or slices of a similar thickness to the beef. Layer the meat in a terrine. Season lightly with pepper, and scatter the spices over the meat. Pour the port and stock over the meat, and place the bay leaf on top. Cover with kitchen foil, and cook in the bottom half of a preheated oven at 180°C/350°F/Gas 4, until the meat is just cooked through and tender.

Remove from the oven and drain off the cooking juices, which can be reserved for another dish. Cover the meat again with foil, weight down, cool and then refrigerate for several hours. The meat can then be thinly sliced if to be used immediately, or it can be covered with clarified butter for use in 2–3 days' time.

Potted Beef and Grouse

The ingredients used in the previous recipe will also make potted meat. Prepare, season and cook the meat as described above.

When cooked, drain off the juices, and put the meat into a processor or mincer with about 115g (4oz) butter and a little of the cooking juices. Mince or process until smooth, and pack into ramekins to be covered with clarified butter, if it is to be served as a starter, or use the meat as a spread for sandwiches.

Cornish Pasty | serves 2

Before the days of school and works canteens, substantial portable meals had to be devised. Pasties made with a firm shortcrust pastry and filled with meat, potatoes and vegetables fitted the bill admirably. The Cornish pasty is probably the best-known survivor of that era, but it was by no means the only one. Lancashire miners, for their 'snap', would take a 'foot', a baked foot-shaped pasty filled with meat (often bacon), potatoes and onion. Forfar bridies from Angus in Scotland resemble Cornish pasties in shape and filling.

Having thought that the recipe for the true Cornish pasty was immutable, I was pleasantly surprised to discover how many variations there are in the fillings. Meat, potatoes, onions and turnips, and various combinations of these ingredients, are most often referred to, but a Cornishman describing school lunches tells how some were filled with meat and potatoes, some with egg and bacon, some with apple and yet another with rabbit. I have also come across recipes which include liver or kidney, and a 1922 recipe from St Ives which includes carrot. In the 1930s a contributor to a collection of traditional English recipes, *Good Things in England*, describes the Cornish pasty with 'pastry joined at the side' and the hoggan made without potato joined across the top. The 'tiddy oggie', however, is a Cornish pasty filled with potatoes. Confusing. Whatever filling you choose, there should be plenty of it, and the pastry well sealed. It was usual to make large pasties, and mark each person's initial at one end of it so that if it was too much to be eaten at one sitting, the leftover portion could be identified at teatime.

I was very lucky to have the chance to watch the expert ladies at Warren's Bakery in St Just filling, rolling and sealing pasties; they worked incredibly fast and neatly. Clearly it takes many years of practice to crimp a pasty properly.

For the pastry
225g (8oz) plain flour
good pinch of salt
115g (4oz) fat (use a mixture of lard and butter)

For the filling
2–3 large potatoes
piece of turnip or swede
225g (8oz) feather or blade steak, cut into small pieces
onion, peeled and chopped (optional)
sea salt and freshly ground black pepper

Sift the flour and salt. Rub in the fat, and mix to a pliable consistency with water. Leave to rest in a cool place while preparing the ingredients for the filling.

Take half the pastry, and roll it into a round, about 5 mm (¼in) thick (use a plate as a guide, if you like). Peel and slice the potato thinly on to the centre of the pastry round, extending to each side to form a base. Slice the turnip thinly on to this, and then put a generous layer of beef over the top, making sure that there is a good piece in each corner. Add a fringe of onion, if using. Season generously with salt and pepper.

Dampen around the edge of the top half-circle of pastry with water. Bring the bottom centre to the top centre to seal firmly, then enclose along to right and left. The finer this sealed edge, the neater will be the crimp. There should now be a neat, fat parcel with no bits poking through. If there are splits or holes, patch them with bits of pastry.

Now do the crimping, from one corner to the other. Make sure your hands are dry. Hold the edge with one hand, and follow with a firm fold down with the other. Hold and fold alternately and swiftly along to the end. Put the pasty on to a piece of buttered paper and slit a hole in the top, to let out the steam. Brush the top with a little milk, and place on a greased baking tray.

Make a second pasty in the same way.

Bake in a preheated oven at 200°C/400°F/Gas6 for 30 minutes, then reduce the heat to 190°C/375°F/Gas5, for a further 30 minutes.

Use the same ingredients to make 4 teatime pasties, using a saucer-size circle, or about a dozen tiny pasties, using a 2.5cm (1in) scone cutter.

Chicken

Not long ago, I received a letter from someone who had just read *The Real Meat Cookbook*. As a poultry meat inspector, he had been involved in the industry for eighteen years and found himself agreeing with what I had written about factory farming. 'Welfare is a big issue,' he wrote, and 'one in my experience, both the industry and the Ministry seem loath to take any responsibility for. Poultry production has become a purely profit-motivated industry and any sort of old-fashioned farming or husbandry attitudes have become obsolete. Apart from the horror of being reared in such intensive and unnatural conditions, the animal has to be transported, often long distances, and finally slaughtered.'

You might expect such sentiments from an ardent campaigner for better food, from a committed vegetarian, from an animal rights activist. But no, this is from someone inside the poultry industry who doesn't like what he sees. His subsequent comments would be hilarious except that they are deeply disturbing: 'The fact that the product is bland and wet seems of little surprise. I was recently told by a MAFF official at a seminar that that was the great thing about chicken; it tastes of nothing; therefore you could add whatever flavour you liked.'

If there really was no alternative to this kind of meat, to cheap, intensively reared chickens, I would have become a vegetarian long ago. But there are farmers all over the country who feel as my correspondent did, when he wrote, 'I strongly believe there is a place for meat in our diet but not at any price.'

As with egg production, there are poultry farmers who rear their birds to very high standards of traditional husbandry, with a feed of grain and natural foraging, plenty of space and shelter, and medication only if and when necessary, not as part of the regular diet.

At Swaddles Green Farm under the Blackdown Hills on the Devon–Somerset border, Bill and Charlotte Reynolds have an organic poultry farm. Ducks and chickens are reared without antibiotic-laced feed, and the Reynoldses explained to me in clear terms the risks associated with these food additives, namely, drug-resistant food-poisoning bacteria, devaluation of critical drugs, and antibiotic residues which pass into the human food-chain.

In an ideal world we would be able to buy our chickens from farms like this. Instead we have to choose from what we are offered. What do all the confusing labels mean on the birds which we see in the supermarkets and butchers' shops? What is a 'farm-fresh chicken', a 'British Farm Chicken'?

Forty-two days, just six weeks old, is the slaughter age for what the British Chicken Information Service describes as 'conventionally reared' chickens. The early slaughter age is possible with modern breeds, which grow rapidly. 'Conventional' rearing allows for a density of twenty to twenty-five birds per square metre. A square metre is a little larger than an opened-out copy of *The Times*. There is no standard size of poultry house, but it can be up to 2,000 metres square, housing 40–50,000 chickens. These are automated units, with feed, lighting and water being controlled by electrical means, so that thousands of birds can be looked after by one person. Technically, these 'conventionally reared' birds (and I do find this expression chilling) are free to move around, but with many thousands more birds packed around them, it is difficult to see how they can move. This is how it is possible to rear cheap chickens, and they will cost around £1 per 450g (1lb), less if frozen and when on special offer. These are the cheapest birds on the market, and are what you are buying under such labels as 'British Farm Chickens'.

You might think that free-range birds had a much better life. Well, up to a point. They are fed a diet of 70 per cent cereal. Only thirteen birds are permitted per square metre, and they must have access to at least one square metre of vegetation-covered ground outdoors. Again, there is no standard size for the poultry house, nor any restriction on the number of such houses per farm. These birds, also rapid-growth breeds, are slaughtered at fifty-six days, or eight weeks, and you can expect to pay about £2 per 450g (1lb) for them.

The label 'traditional free-range' indicates a traditional breed, which grows more slowly than the modern breeds. They are slaughtered at eighty-one days. Their regime provides for no more than twelve birds per square metre in a house no more than 400 metres square. That is still 4,400 birds in one hen house. They are fed a diet of 70 per cent cereal, have access (at least two square metres per bird) to grassy open-air runs, from the age of six weeks onwards, that is, for thirty-nine days.

The label 'free-range total freedom' requires the same standards, with the addition of access to roam outside in an unfenced area. These birds will cost closer to £2 to £2.50 per 450g (1lb).

Organic chickens are available for a little more. They will have the symbol of the Soil Association, or one of the other approved certification bodies, such as Organic Farmers and Growers Ltd or the Biodynamic Association, on the packaging, which will reassure you that the birds have been reared to a high standard of animal husbandry, fed on a largely, and sometimes wholly, organic diet, and inspected regularly. Following EU legislation, only food produced by a registered organic producer may be sold as organic.

We also see corn-fed chickens. Some are labelled 'free-range' but many are 'conventionally reared'. Neither bird is fed on an exclusively corn-based diet. And the yellow colour of the flesh and fat can be induced by adding a colourant such as beta-carotene to the chicken feed.

A really fine bird is, contrary to the MAFF official's views, full of flavour and with a good chewy texture. Roasting it will show it off at its best, quite worthy of one of your finer bottles of claret or burgundy.

Roast Chicken with Stuffing | serves 4–6

a 2.3kg (5lb) free-range organic chicken
1 bay leaf
2 cloves
½ lemon
sea salt and freshly ground black pepper

Remove any excess fat from the body cavity of the chicken. Spike the bay leaf with the cloves, and tuck this into the cavity. Rub the bird all over with the cut lemon, squeezing the juice over the bird, then put the half-lemon inside the body cavity. Season lightly with salt and pepper inside and out, and place the chicken *on its side* on a rack in a roasting tin.

Roast in a preheated oven at 200°C/400°F/Gas 6 for 35 minutes. Turn it on to its other side, and roast for a further 25 minutes. Finally, turn the chicken on its back, and roast for a further 20 minutes or so. The juices which are released when you pierce the inner thigh with a skewer should be clear and not pink. Transfer the chicken to a serving platter. Skim the fat from the pan juices, and transfer them to a saucepan.

To make a little gravy, add a splash or two of the wine you will serve with the meal, and if you wish, thicken it with a little potato flour, cornflour or ordinary flour. For a creamy gravy, add the milk in which the stuffing ingredients are cooked. While the bird is roasting, the stuffing can also be cooking, in the oven.

Celery, Almond and Dried Fruit Stuffing

serves 5–6

4–6 slices of day-old bread, left out to dry
2–3 celery stalks, trimmed and chopped
1 small onion, peeled and diced
1 clove
1 cinnamon stick
1 bay leaf
150ml (¼ pint) milk
85–115g (3–4oz) flaked almonds
115g (4oz) dried apricots, finely chopped
sea salt and freshly ground black pepper
1 free-range egg, lightly beaten

Tear the bread into small pieces, with or without the crusts, as you prefer. Simmer the celery, onion and spices in the milk for 5 minutes. Discard the spices, and strain the vegetables. You can keep the milk if you wish to make a cream gravy for the chicken.

Mix the bread, vegetables, almonds, apricots and seasoning, and bind with the egg. Spoon into a greased ovenproof container, such as a soufflé dish. Smooth the surface, and bake the stuffing in the bottom half of the oven for about an hour.

Note

I like to serve the chicken just with its gravy and stuffing, and follow it with a green salad. If you prefer to serve vegetables with the chicken, I suggest beans, broccoli or cabbage, together with a baked or roasted root vegetable, such as parsnip or celeriac.

This is not, of course, the end of the chicken. The carcase, while it will not produce a sparkling, restaurant-type clear stock, will make a very good base for a soup. Simmer it gently with a celery top, a slice of ginger, if you wish, the outer layer of a small onion, and a few peppercorns. After a couple of hours, strain, cool, and chill the broth, or reduce it, chill it, and freeze it for later use. If you want to use it the next day, also use any leftover scraps of chicken to make this lovely soup, creamy, intriguingly spicy, and deeply satisfying.

Chicken and Artichoke Soup | serves 4–6

1 onion, peeled and sliced
55g (2oz) unsalted butter
1 tablespoon plain flour
675g (1½lb) Jerusalem artichokes, well scrubbed and sliced
freshly grated nutmeg
pinch each of ground cloves, cardamom, cinnamon and white pepper
300ml (½ pint) milk, semi-skimmed or skimmed
850ml (1½ pints) chicken stock
sea salt, to taste
shreds of cooked chicken

To finish
cream or fresh chopped herbs

In a large, heavy saucepan, sweat the onion in the butter until soft. Stir in the flour, artichokes and spices, and gradually add the milk. Bring to the boil, then simmer until the vegetables are soft. Blend until smooth with the stock. Bring back to the boil, adjust the seasoning, and stir in the chicken. Serve in heated bowls with a swirl of cream or a sprinkling of herbs.

Stove-top Chicken with Leeks and Potatoes

serves 4–6

While whole roast chicken is hard to beat, this recipe and the next one use different parts of the chicken: an easy stove-top dish for a family supper using thighs and drumsticks, and a more elegant dish using the breasts, mean you will need to buy 2 birds.

thighs, wings and drumsticks from 2 free-range organic chickens
70ml (⅛ pint) olive oil
900g (2lb) potatoes, peeled and cut into 2.5–5cm (1–2in) pieces
900g (2lb) leeks, trimmed, sliced and washed thoroughly
dry white wine or broth, to moisten
sea salt and freshly ground black pepper

Fry the chicken in a third of the oil, and cook for 20 minutes. Fry the potatoes separately in another third of the oil, and also cook for 20 minutes. Stir both pans at intervals to prevent the food from sticking.

In one large frying pan, fry the leeks in the rest of the oil for 5–10 minutes, then add the chicken and potatoes. Cook for 10–15 minutes more, uncovered, until the chicken and potatoes are tender. Moisten with wine or broth, if it looks like drying out.

To serve, pile on to a heated serving platter and season lightly with salt and pepper.

Baked Stuffed Chicken Breasts with Cucumber

serves 4

4 free-range organic chicken breasts, off the bone
2 large cucumbers
1 tablespoon salt
25g (1oz) unsalted butter
4 tablespoons dry white wine or chicken stock
sea salt and freshly ground black pepper
1 tablespoon chopped fresh dill, plus a few fresh fronds to garnish

For the stuffing
4 free-range chicken fillets
2 free-range organic chicken livers
25–55g (1–2oz) flat-leaf parsley
3 tablespoons double cream, clotted cream, or crème fraiche
sea salt and freshly ground black pepper
freshly grated nutmeg

Remove the skin and any fat from the chicken breasts, and with a sharp knife make a pocket in them. Shave the skin off the cucumber in thin strips, and cut the cucumber in half lengthways. Scoop out and discard the seeds, and slice the cucumber as thinly as possible.

Place in a colander, sprinkle with salt, and mix with your

hands to get all the cucumber salty. Leave to degorge over a bowl for an hour or so, before rinsing thoroughly and drying in a clean tea-towel.

Meanwhile prepare the stuffing. Remove the sinew from the chicken fillets. Trim the chicken livers of any threads and green parts tainted by the gall bladder.

Roughly chop the livers and the fillets, and blend them in a food processor until smooth. Rub this mixture through a sieve. Blanch the parsley leaves in boiling water, and refresh under cold running water. Dry thoroughly, and chop very finely. Mix into the chicken stuffing, together with the cream, salt, pepper and nutmeg. Spoon the mixture into the chicken breasts, and secure with wooden cocktail sticks.

Fry the chicken breasts in half the butter on both sides, cover partially, and cook until juices run clear. Place the chicken on a warm serving dish. Add the wine or stock to the pan juices, season lightly with salt and pepper, scrape up any residues, and add the dill. Cook for a minute or two, and pour over the chicken.

Fry the cucumber in the remaining butter until wilted and bright green. Arrange it around the chicken and serve.

Chicken, Vegetable and Herb Cobbler

serves 6–8

This recipe is another version of my favourite cobbler. I like to make this in the summer when there are plenty of tender young vegetables about.

24 pickling onions or 12 shallots, peeled
1.35kg (3lb) free-range organic chicken, both dark and light meat, off the bone and diced
2 tablespoons sunflower oil
1 tablespoon plain flour
½ bottle dry white wine
150ml (¼ pint) chicken stock
1 bay leaf

For the vegetables
A selection from the following, about 675–900g (1½–2lb) in all:
green beans
small carrots
sweetcorn
courgettes
small potatoes
button mushrooms

For the herb cobbler

25g (1oz) fresh parsley, chervil and oregano

½ teaspoon coarse sea salt

280g (10oz) self-raising flour

1 teaspoon baking powder

85g (3oz) lard or butter, chilled and diced

about 150ml (¼ pint) buttermilk or plain yoghurt, thinned with water to the consistency of cream

In a flameproof casserole with a lid, fry the onions or shallots and chicken in the oil until golden-brown. Sprinkle on the flour, and stir in to absorb any extra oil. Add a quarter of the wine, and bring to the boil, stirring up any residues in the casserole.

Pour in the rest of the wine and the stock, add the bay leaf, bring to the boil, cover, and turn down the heat. Simmer gently for 20 minutes, then add the vegetables, and cook for a further 20–30 minutes, until the vegetables are tender. Courgettes, corn kernels and mushrooms will, of course, take much less cooking and should be added towards the end.

To make the cobbler, strip the leaves from the herb stalks, and crush them with the salt in a mortar and pestle. Sift the flour with the baking powder, cut in the fat, then rub together. Add the herbs, and stir in enough buttermilk to bind the mixture to a soft dough. Roll out and cut into rounds.

Remove the lid from the casserole, arrange the scones round the top, and bake in a preheated oven at 180°C/350°F/Gas 4 for about 15 minutes. Serve from the casserole.

Duck Breasts with a Honey, Thyme and Cider Glaze | serves 8

8 duck breasts
115ml (4 fl oz) dry cider
85g (3oz) honey
2–3 sprigs of fresh thyme
1–2 tablespoons Somerset cider brandy
450g (1lb) onions, peeled and sliced
300ml (½ pint) duck stock
salt and freshly ground black pepper
good pinch of freshly grated nutmeg
2–3 tablespoons double cream

For the garnish
extra thyme or other fresh herbs

Score the fat on the duck breasts in small lozenges. Remove the arrow-shaped fillet loosely attached underneath the duck breast and use for another dish. Bring the cider, honey, thyme and brandy to the boil. Allow to cool, then brush over the duck skin and place skin side down in a shallow dish. Leave overnight.

Cook the onions in the duck stock until soft, then sieve, season with salt, pepper and nutmeg, and whisk in the cream. Cook the duck in a heavy frying pan, about 7–8 minutes on the skin side, and 4–5 minutes on the other side, to give a well-coloured crisp skin.

Drain off all the fat before serving the meat with the onion sauce.

Note

A cake of grated potato and celeriac goes very well with this, as do glazed baby beetroots and turnips in apple juice. When I served this dish at the Café Royal we also minced the duck fillet, mixed it with herbs and breadcrumbs, and used this forcemeat to stuff cabbage leaves rolled into balls.

Duckling Casserole

serves 6,plus another meal of duck breasts for 4

Here is a duck recipe for the winter, when root vegetables are at their best.

2 × 2.3kg (5lb) ducklings
2 onions, peeled and sliced
4 cloves
1 bay leaf
1 sprig of fresh thyme
300ml (½ pint) dry white wine
450g (1lb) prepared root vegetables

For the stock
1 celery stalk
1 slice of fresh root ginger (optional)
1 bay leaf

Remove the wishbone from each duckling, then, with a sharp knife, remove each breast. Reserve these for another meal – they can be marinated and refrigerated.

Cut off the wings and the legs. Divide the leg joints into thigh and drumstick, and cut the wings into 3 obvious joints. The smallest wing joints and the carcases, chopped up, go into a large pan of water with a piece of celery stalk, a slice of ginger if you have it and a bay leaf to make stock. But first, remove as much of the skin and fat as possible from carcases and leg joints. Put this into a casserole or ovenproof dish, cover and place in the bottom of the oven to melt. This will take at least as long as the casserole takes to cook. When all the fat has been rendered, strain into a container, and refrigerate when cool.

To make the casserole, fry the onions in a spoonful of duck fat, then brown the meat. Add the cloves, herbs and wine. Bring to simmering point, add the vegetables, cover and cook in the middle of a preheated oven at 180°C/350°F/Gas 4 for about 45 minutes, then turn the oven down to 150°C/ 300°F/Gas 2 and cook for a further 1½ hours, until the duck is tender.

Note

Duck fat is excellent in pastry and scone-making and for frying potatoes. I fry potatoes perhaps once or twice a year, and when I do, I like something tasty to fry them in. The remaining bits of skin and meat in the pan can be chopped, transferred to a frying pan and crisped up to serve as lardons with a frisée salad. Thus, nothing is wasted. If you have got giblets with the ducklings, put the neck in the stockpot, and the heart, gizzard and liver with the casserole.

I like to cook small parsnips with the duck, but carrots, turnips, potatoes and chunks of celeriac are equally good. So too are sliced leeks. Once when I served this, a purée of celeriac and a carefully hoarded can of Rodel petit pois were excellent accompaniments.

Spring Duckling Stew | serves 6–8

Here is a spring or summer version of the previous recipe.

2.75kg (6lb) duck, jointed into 8 pieces
450g (1lb) new potatoes
450g (1lb) small purple and white turnips, or navets
450g (1lb) young carrots, peeled, if necessary
6 garlic cloves, peeled (optional)
1 bouquet garni, made of 2–3 parsley stalks, 1 bay leaf, a sprig of fresh tarragon and a sprig of fresh thyme
300ml (½ pint) duck or chicken stock
225g (8oz) green beans, trimmed
2 bunches of spring onions, trimmed
sea salt and freshly ground black pepper

Heat a heavy-based frying pan with a lid, and put the duck pieces in it, skin side down, with the fat on. Cook gently until the fat runs free. Then raise the heat to brown the pieces, turn them over, and brown the other side. Pour off the fat.

Put the potatoes, turnips, carrots, and garlic if using it into the pan, cutting up the vegetables to the same size, if necessary, to ensure even cooking. Tuck in the bouquet garni. Pour on the stock, bring to the boil, cover, and simmer gently for 30 minutes. Add the green beans and spring onions, and simmer for a further 20–25 minutes, until both meat and vegetables are tender. Season to taste and serve.

Note

If you can also get fresh peas and broad beans, add a few of these about 5 minutes before the end of cooking time. The casserole needs no other accompaniment. A green salad and cheese will follow it perfectly, before serving a pudding.

Tom's Cornish Casserole of Guinea-fowl and Sausage | serves 4–6

This dish is marvellous. Tom, my husband, had it ready for me one evening after a long day away from the Mill. He served a delicious 1992 Meursault with it.

1 free-range guinea-fowl, jointed (use the back and wings to make 300ml (½ pint) stock)
2 tablespoons extra virgin olive oil
1 onion, peeled and sliced
3–4 garlic cloves, peeled and crushed
300ml (½ pint) cider, scrumpy, or good dry white wine
2 tablespoons grain mustard
1 teaspoon hot chilli mustard
450g (1lb) good-quality pork sausages
chopped fresh mint
sea salt and freshly ground black pepper

Fry the guinea-fowl in the oil until just browned, then add the onion and garlic. Pour on the cider or wine, bring to the boil, and stir in the mustards. Lower the heat, and simmer for 40 minutes or so.

Meanwhile, quarter the sausages, and fry them in a non-stick pan to get rid of as much fat as possible. Drain and wipe the sausages, and add to the casserole. Cook for a few minutes together, stir in some mint and season to taste with salt and pepper. Stock can be added if the casserole shows signs of drying out.

Pot-roast Guinea-fowl, Stuffed with Herbs and Garlic, with Onion Sauce | serves 4

1 free-range guinea-fowl
fresh herbs such as tarragon, chervil, basil, flat-leaf parsley, thyme as available
½ lemon
sea salt and freshly ground black pepper
1–2 heads of garlic, new season if possible
55g (2oz) butter
1 onion, peeled and thinly sliced
1 measure of cognac
75ml (⅛ pint) dry white wine
2 tablespoons cream (optional)

Gently ease the skin away from the breasts and thighs of the guinea-fowl, inserting your finger between skin and flesh at the neck end of the bird. Push the tarragon, chervil, basil or flat-leaf parsley under the skin, as well as small tender sprigs of thyme. Pare off thin strips of lemon zest, and put this inside the cavity, together with any extra herbs. Squeeze the lemon juice, rub over the bird, and season it lightly inside and out.

Peel all the garlic cloves, and in a deep flameproof casserole, fry them in the butter with the onion slices for a few minutes, without letting them brown. Turn the guinea-fowl in the hot butter, pour on the cognac, and flame it. Add the wine, cover with a lid, and cook the guinea-fowl in a preheated oven at 175°C/325°F/Gas3 for about 1½ hours.

Transfer the bird, whole or jointed as you prefer, to a warm serving dish. Skim the fat from the cooking juices through a sieve, and bring to the boil. Add more seasoning, if necessary, cream if you like, or reduce over the heat if you prefer a thicker sauce. Serve with the bird.

Note

The guinea-fowl carcase, broken up, covered with water, to which you have added a piece of celery stalk, a slice of ginger and a few peppercorns, will make a very good stock for later use.

Bread, Pies, Pasties and Puddings

We filmed at Crowdy Mill in Harbertonford, Devon, which Don and Ann Barnes had restored to working order. Don thought the mill wheel was a good few hundred years old. The millstones, set in pairs, the runner and the bedstone, are 4 feet across, and each weighs about a ton. You might think that the local stone would be used for the millstone, but Derbyshire grit, also called millstone grit, and French burr are the hardest stones and generally used. These are what produce stone-ground flour. The surface of the stone is cut to make a grinding surface, first into segments, or 'harps', and then into 'furrows'. The 'land' on either side of the furrow also has its surface chipped. And then, of course, the second stone must be cut as a mirror image. The millstones used today are dressed, or cut, just as they would have been when the mill was first built.

I love the bakeries in the West Country, with their heavy cakes, lardy cakes, congress tarts and saffron cakes. And these are not just quaint treats for tourists. One of the local grocers in Lostwithiel always has saffron and fresh yeast, and she told me that home baking is alive and well, certainly for yeast cakes.

The bread from Lostwithiel bakery was so good that I rarely bothered to make my own. Occasionally, though, the baker would let me have some flour if I'd run out. This, of course, was strong flour, the type most associated with commercial bread-making. But I also baked several batches in the Aga with fresh stone-ground flour from Crowdy Mill (now closed), made from soft English organic wheat. I have found that the secret with bread-making is to make it work to your timetable, rather than the other way round; that way you can be quite relaxed about it, and the whole process does not become a tyranny.

I was curious to try out the Crowdy Mill flour and the Aga and I had good results from both. Then I really got into a baking mood and made prune and walnut baps with a mixture of unbleached and wholemeal flour, and then, because the oven temperature still seemed high, I made dozens of spice biscuits, not unlike Cornish Fairings, but without the ginger. Ah well, I thought, I would be back in my small urban North London kitchen soon, so I decided to make the most of the Mill's large, light and airy kitchen, and all the wonderful fresh food I was able to buy here.

White Loaf | makes a 1kg (2lb) loaf

450g (1lb) stone-ground flour
2 teaspoons salt
2 teaspoons fast-action easy-blend yeast granules
2 tablespoons olive oil
generous 300ml (½ pint) warm water

In a large bowl mix the dry ingredients. Make a well in the centre, and pour in the liquid ingredients. Draw the flour into the centre and mix well, until the dough leaves the sides of the bowl. You can, of course, make the dough in a food processor.

Turn on to a floured work top, and knead for 10 minutes. Shape the dough, and put it into a lightly greased 1kg (2lb) loaf tin. Cover loosely with lightly oiled clingfilm, and leave to rise in a warm place for about an hour until doubled in size.

Bake in a preheated oven at 200°C/400°F/Gas6 for about 30 minutes. Turn the loaf on to a wire rack, and leave to cool completely before slicing.

Note

In making your own recipes, remember the proportions:

– 1 teaspoon salt to about 225g (8oz) flour

– By volume, about half liquid to flour

450g (1lb) flour will make 12–18 bread rolls; these will bake at the same temperature in about 15 minutes.

Flavourings can be mixed in just before you knead the dough. Try: onion and rosemary, spring onion and cheese, sundried tomatoes, chopped olives.

Enriched, sweet bread can be made by adding 2 tablespoons dried skimmed milk powder, 2–3 tablespoons sugar or honey, and 2 free-range eggs. To this, you can add cinnamon and walnuts, chopped dried apricots and almonds, dates and brazil nuts, mixed dried fruit and candied peel, or saffron and sunflower seeds.

Cider Bread | makes 3 loaves

1 tablespoon salt
1.35kg (3lb) strong white flour
25kg (1oz) fresh yeast
1 teaspoon caster sugar or honey
850ml (1½ pints) farm cider

Sift the flour and salt into a large bowl, and make a well in the centre. Cream the yeast and sugar or honey, stir in a third of the cider, and pour into the well. Gather in enough of the flour to make a thin batter without breaking the flour 'wall'. Sprinkle some of the flour over the top, and let the yeast work for about 20 minutes until the batter breaks through the surface. Stir the yeast mixture into the flour, adding the rest of the cider until you have a workable mass of dough.

Turn on to a floured work top, and knead for 20 minutes. Put the bread into an oiled bowl, cover with oiled kitchen foil or clingfilm, and leave to rise for a couple of hours in a warm place. Or let it rise slowly in the refrigerator for up to 24 hours.

Turn the dough on to a floured work top again, and give it a second kneading, but only for about 5 minutes this time. Shape into loaves, and put into oiled tins or on trays, cover once more, and leave to rise for about 45 minutes.

Bake the loaves in a preheated oven at 200°C/400°F/Gas6 for about 40 minutes. Turn the loaves on to a wire rack, and leave to cool completely before slicing.

Lardy Cake

1 teaspoon caster sugar
300ml (½ pint) warm water
1 tablespoon fast-action easy-blend yeast granules
450g (1lb) strong white flour
2 teaspoons salt
225g (8oz) lard, chilled
115g (4oz) mixed raisins and sultanas
115g (4oz) caster sugar
½ teaspoon ground nutmeg, cloves, cinnamon or allspice

Make a plain dough by mixing the teaspoon of sugar and water in a bowl and sprinkling the yeast on top. When it has begun to froth, mix it with the flour, salt and 25g (1oz) of the lard cut into the flour, in a large bowl. Knead until the dough is elastic and smooth. Place in an oiled bowl, and cover with clingfilm or a damp tea-towel. Leave to rise in a warm place until doubled in size. Knock it back, and, on a floured work top, roll it out to a rectangle 5mm–1cm (¼–½ in) thick.

Dot the surface with a third of the lard at regular intervals, and sprinkle with a third of the fruit and sugar. Fold the bottom third of the dough up and the top third down so that it is folded into three. Give the dough a turn so that the short edges are at the top and bottom. Roll the dough out as before, dot with more lard, fruit and sugar, fold, and turn and repeat the process once more, this time sprinkling on the spice with the fruit and sugar.

Roll the dough out to fit a 20 × 25 cm (8 × 10 in) greased cake tin. Score into squares or rectangles, cover with a damp tea-towel or oiled clingfilm, and leave in a warm place to prove for 20–30 minutes. Bake in a preheated oven at 220°C/425°F/Gas 7 for 35–40 minutes, or until golden-brown. Remove from the tin, dust with sugar and leave to cool on a wire rack. Lardy cake is traditionally broken into pieces to serve, not cut.

Saffron

The West Country's Very Own Gold

Cape Cornwall, barely a mile shorter than Land's End, might miss the distinction of being the westernmost tip of our islands, but it also misses the hordes of visitors. It is wild and bleak and almost overwhelming. Down here is the last relic, the tall chimney, of the Cape Cornwall tin mine, which closed in 1870. Tin mining in Cornwall goes back thousands of years; without Cornish tin, would there have been a Bronze Age?

St Just is England's westernmost town. A centre of tin mining in Victorian times, it is the home of Warrens, bakers since 1860, and now being run by fourth- and fifth-generation Warrens. Saffron cakes and tea treats are their local specialities; the former are now sent by post to homesick Cornishmen all over the world.

Legend has it that saffron was brought into Cornwall by the Phoenicians who came to trade for Cornish tin. A nice legend, but unfortunately there is no evidence to suggest that the Phoenicians ever reached the British Isles. Indeed, Portugal is the furthest north they are thought to have reached, and there was plenty of tin for the Phoenicians in the Iberian Peninsula. It is more likely to have been introduced by the Romans and then brought back from the Middle East by the Crusaders, and later by pilgrims.

Saffron has been a precious spice in our store cupboards since the earliest times. These slender, dry red filaments, the stigma of the autumn-flowering crocus, almost insignificant in themselves, add a rich colour, fragrance and inimitable flavour to food, qualities which were much prized in medieval times throughout Europe and not just in Spain. Now most of the saffron we buy is probably from La Mancha in Spain, although saffron also comes from Egypt, Greece, Iran, Kashmir, India and Morocco. Unfortunately, it is also very easy to imitate the appearance of dried saffron, though not its flavour, with the dried petals of the safflower, a member of the thistle family, from which safflower oil is derived. But for centuries saffron was grown at Saffron Walden in Essex.

Saffron was harvested and sold at the great fair in Saffron Walden on 21 October and at Newport Fair on 17 November. It was always scarce and expensive and used to be a traditional gift from the Corporation of Saffron Walden to royal visitors to Audley End in the sixteenth and seventeenth centuries. In 1561 a pound of saffron cost £1 5s; in 1661 £3 10s, and in 1717 £4 11s was paid for saffron to present to King George I. There is a Cornish saying, 'as dear as saffron', and in the Philadelphia commodities market in the 1700s saffron was 'worth its weight in gold'. Over a quarter of a million saffron flowers are harvested, and picked over by hand, to extract enough filaments to produce 450g (1lb) of saffron!

At one time, saffron was used to colour butter and cheese. Shakespeare refers in *A Winter's Tale* to its use for colouring pear pies. Saffron cakes, buns and biscuits are still made in Devon,

Cornwall, Northumberland and Ireland, especially at Eastertime. When a friend of mine, John Humphries, who imports saffron, was married, his wedding cake was iced in a glorious golden icing, coloured with saffron. He has also used saffron successfully, if somewhat expensively, to dye table linen, and has written a very good book, *The Essential Saffron Companion*, on the story of saffron and its many uses, culinary and other.

I use saffron a good deal in my cooking, and have included in the book many recipes, both savoury and sweet, using saffron. Although we are more accustomed today to use saffron in risottos, paellas and bouillabaisse, there are a number of traditional English recipes using saffron. One of the oldest I have come across is for an early form of cheesecake, using honey, saffron and soft cheese, mixed with eggs and baked in a pastry case. It was while talking to a friend who was brought up in Cornwall that I was first inspired to try my hand at saffron buns many years ago. You can imagine my delight, then, to be able to spend time in Warren's Bakery in St Just, as well as in private kitchens, watching the golden dough being prepared.

Numerous recipes are to be found, some using the rubbing-in method, some the melted method. Hilary Spurling in *Elinor Fettiplace's Receipt Book* gives an Elizabethan version in which the butter is melted in sack or sherry. Hannah Glasse's eighteenth-century recipe offers the option of including caraway seeds, but she writes, 'I think it rather better without.' I do too. On the other hand, I like her suggestion of rosewater, another favourite English ingredient of the time, and one found in some of the many Cornish versions of saffron cake still in existence.

Brochie's Saffron Buns | makes about 2 dozen

These buns are best of all served warm and freshly baked.

1 tablespoon fast-action easy-blend yeast granules
up to 450ml (¾ pint) warm milk
115g (4oz) caster sugar
good pinch (about ½ teaspoon or 2g) saffron strands
225g (8oz) butter, lard, or a mixture of the two
675g (1½lb) strong plain flour
225g (8oz) seedless raisins or sultanas
55–85g (2–3oz) mixed candied peel
1–2 tablespoons rosewater (optional)

Sprinkle the dried yeast on 150ml (¼ pint) of the milk, together with 1 teaspoon sugar, in a jug, and let it work for 10–15 minutes, until frothy. Soak the saffron in 2–3 tablespoons very hot water. Rub the fat into the flour in a large bowl, stir in the rest of the sugar, the fruit and mixed peel. Make a well in the centre, and pour in the yeast, the rosewater, if using, and the saffron liquid. Combine to a dough, adding more warm milk as necessary. Knead on a floured work top until smooth, and place in an oiled bowl. Cover with a clean, damp tea-towel, and leave the dough to rise for an hour or so in a draught-free place.

Knock the dough back, and shape into buns. Put these on a greased baking sheet, cover again, and leave them to rise for a further 30–40 minutes. Bake in a preheated oven at 180°C/ 350°F/Gas 4 for 40–45 minutes.

Note

The buns can, if you wish, be brushed with an egg and milk glaze before baking.

Quick Saffron Bread

makes a 900g (2lb) loaf or 2 smaller loaves

a few saffron strands
150ml (¼ pint) boiling water
675g (1½lb) strong white flour
2 teaspoons salt
1 sachet (7g) fast-action easy-blend yeast granules
4 tablespoons extra virgin olive oil
300ml (½ pint) cold water

Put the saffron into a bowl, and pour on a little of the boiling water. In a large bowl or food processor, mix the dry ingredients, and then add all the liquids, including the oil and saffron liquid, mixed together. When the dough is thoroughly mixed, knead it for 10 minutes on a floured work top until smooth and elastic. Divide and shape as appropriate, and place in greased tins, or on a greased baking sheet if making bread rolls, a cottage loaf or plait. Cover with a damp tea-towel, and leave to rise in a warm place until doubled in volume.

Bake in a preheated oven at 230°C/450°F/Gas 8 for about 35–40 minutes for a large loaf, 30 minutes for 2 small ones, and 15–20 minutes for bread rolls.

Saffron Bread and Butter Pudding | serves 8–10

You can make this with bought saffron cake, sliced saffron buns, or my Quick Saffron Bread (see previous recipe). If you use the latter, you might want to sprinkle a handful of raisins or sultanas, two or three tablespoons of sugar and some chopped mixed peel between the layers of buttered bread.

sliced saffron bread, liberally buttered and cut into triangles
4 free-range eggs
300ml (½ pint) each full-cream milk and single cream

Liberally butter an ovenproof dish, and lay the pieces of bread in it. Beat the eggs, milk and cream, pour over the bread, and leave to stand for 20 minutes or so before baking in a preheated oven at 180°C/350°F/Gas 4 for 35–40 minutes.

Fried Saffron Bread | serves 2–4

This rich and delightful version of French toast makes a perfect quick pudding.

1 free-range egg
150ml (¼ pint) dry or medium cider
4 slices of saffron bread
55g (2oz) unsalted butter

To serve
clotted cream
West Country honey

Beat the egg and cider in a shallow basin, and in it dip the saffron bread, making sure it is well coated. Fry in the butter until crisp, and serve hot with a dollop of chilled clotted cream and some honey.

Saffron, Brie and Honey Tart | serves 4–6

pinch of saffron strands
225g (8oz) shortcrust pastry
175g (6oz) mild ripe Brie or similar cheese
225g (8oz) curd cheese
3 tablespoons honey
4–5 tablespoons milk
85g (3oz) demerara sugar
3 free-range eggs

Soak the saffron strands for 20 minutes in a tablespoon of hot water. Roll out the pastry, and line a 25cm (10 in) rimmed pie plate. Use the trimmings to decorate the rim with pastry leaves or a plait, if liked. Prick the pastry all over with a fork. Line with greaseproof paper, fill with baking beans, and bake blind in a preheated oven at 190°C/375°F/Gas 5 for 15–20 minutes.

Put the curd cheese into a bowl, remove the rind from the Brie, and mix thoroughly with the curd cheese. Melt the honey with the milk. Mix the honey, saffron liquid and sugar with the cheese, and beat in the eggs. Pour the mixture carefully into the pie dish, and bake in the preheated oven at190°C/375°F/ Gas3, and bake for a further 20 minutes or so. Serve warm or cold, dusted with a little icing sugar, and with or without clotted cream.

Saffron and Honey Custards | serves 4–6

600ml (1 pint) single or double cream
pinch of saffron strands
4 free-range eggs
1 tablespoon caster sugar

To serve
clear honey
flaked almonds (optional)

Put the cream into a saucepan with the saffron strands. Bring to the boil, and pour over the eggs beaten with the sugar, stirring continuously. Put 4–6 ramekin dishes in a roasting tin and pour in enough water to come halfway up the sides of the ramekins. Pour the mixture into them, cover with a piece of kitchen foil, and bake in the middle of a preheated oven at 175°C/325°F/Gas 3 for about 30 minutes, or until a knifepoint inserted into the middle comes out clean.

Cool and refrigerate for 2–3 hours, or overnight. To serve, spoon a little clear honey over the custards, and, if you wish, scatter on flaked almonds.

Junket

Junket is a smooth, cool, milky pudding, something that you either love or loathe. I was never subjected to it at school, so I see junket as a very agreeable ending to a summer meal. Offer it to some people, however, and you will be met with squeaks of horror, as they recall boarding-school mealtime traumas.

In Anglo-Norman times junket was a soft, fresh cheese, so called after the *jonquet* or basket made from rushes (*jonques*) in which it was drained. And, indeed, making an unsweetened junket is still the first step to a homemade soft cheese. Once it has set, you spoon the solids into a sieve, colander or pierced mould lined with a cheesecloth. The whey will drain off, and the curds will be left behind to be pressed into a round or cylinder.

I like a simple junket best, just lightly sweetened, and served, when it has set, with a thin layer of cream poured on top and a sprinkling of freshly grated nutmeg. A tablespoon of brandy or rum might be stirred in with the sugar. When junket was more popular, or at least more often served, flavourings would be used to ring the changes. Thus, rosewater, orange-flower water or coffee-flavoured junkets would be served. For the latter, I would suggest a little Tia Maria with Camp coffee essence to give the right depth of flavour.

Rennet is the ingredient used to curdle the milk, and it is sold in liquid form or in tablets. These are often already flavoured. If either has been stored too long, some of the potency will be lost. Because rennet is derived from an animal product, the fourth stomach of the calf, it is not suitable for use in vegetarian cookery, and a vegetarian alternative should be sought from a specialist shop. Herbs, such as lady's bedstraw, used to be used for this purpose but often gave the finished dish a bitter flavour. Whichever coagulating agent you use, it is important to follow the direction.

It goes almost without saying that junket is not worth making unless you use good-quality, fresh, creamy milk. Those lucky enough to get raw milk will make a good junket. Otherwise, look for gold top, the Guernsey or Jersey milk that has at least 4 per cent fat.

A honey-sweetened saffron junket makes an unusual ending to a meal – the junket traditional, the flavourings modern in application. Honey really is the perfect sweetener for saffron-flavoured desserts, whether creams, custards, pies or cakes.

Saffron and Honey Junket | serves 4–6

pinch of saffron strands, soaked in 2 tablespoons boiling water
600ml (1 pint) full-cream milk
1 tablespoon honey
1 teaspoon rennet essence
150ml (¼ pint) whipping cream (optional)

Warm the saffron liquid, milk and honey to blood heat, no more. Remove from the heat, and stir in the rennet essence. Carefully pour into a bowl (glass for preference), and leave at room temperature until the junket has set. After that, it can be refrigerated until required. If you like, spoon a layer of cream over the top before serving.

Clotted Cream

It is still possible to buy unpasteurized clotted cream in the West Country, made in the traditional way by farmers' wives in small, cool dairies attached to the farmhouse. This must be one of the great glories of our national culinary heritage and deserving of protection. I have been told to try it on toasted saffron bread. 'Thunder and Lightning' also sounds good – Cornish splits, spread thickly with cream, over which a spoonful of black treacle is trickled.

Jersey and Guernsey cows provide the richest and tastiest milk, but South Devons produce good milk as well as excellent beef. It is lovely to see the sloping cliffside meadows dotted with herds of this traditional breed, their rich, brown coats catching the sunlight between the clouds.

Caramelized Clotted Cream Rice Pudding

serves 4–6

85g (3oz) pudding rice
1 vanilla pod
600ml (1 pint) full-cream milk
caster sugar, to taste
150ml (¼ pint) whipping cream
150ml (¼ pint) clotted cream

Cook the rice and vanilla pod in the milk until the grains are tender. Remove the vanilla pod, split it, and scrape the seeds into the pudding. Stir in the sugar while the mixture is still hot, and allow it to cool. Whip the whipping cream, fold it in, and spoon the mixture into the ramekins. Chill.

Spread the clotted cream on top of the pudding. Sprinkle on a layer of sugar to cover the surface, and put under a hot grill until it melts and caramelizes. Remove from the heat, and refrigerate.

Note

You can achieve a similar effect by cooking the sugar until it just caramelizes, and then pouring it over the chilled pudding. It should set to a nice glossy, brittle surface. Or use a blow-torch.

Quince and Apple Fool | serves 4–6

Apples and pears are interchangeable in this and the next few recipes, which make the most of our orchard fruit.

1 quince
3–4 well-flavoured apples, such as Russets or Coxes
150ml (¼ pint) mead or cider
2–3 cloves
honey, to taste
300ml (½ pint) double cream, whipped, or homemade custard

Wipe the quince, and core and chop it. (The apples take less time to cook and are added later.) Simmer the quince with the mead or cider and the cloves until almost tender. Core and quarter the apples, and add to the pan. Cook until tender. Drain off any excess juice, keeping it for another dish, and rub the fruit pulp through a sieve. If you have used cider, add honey to sweeten. When the fruit is cold, fold in the cream or custard, and spoon into glasses. Serve with crisp, spicy biscuits.

Apple and Mint Pudding | serves 4

450g (1lb) apples
sugar, to taste
85–115g (3–4oz) butter, softened
sliced white bread
150ml (¼ pint) double cream
150ml (¼ pint) sweet sherry
2 sprigs of fresh mint
lemon juice
6 tablespoons apricot jam

For decoration
25g (1oz) flaked almonds, lightly toasted

Peel, core and roughly chop the apples, and cook for 2–3 minutes with just enough sugar to sweeten them. Butter the slices of bread, and cut each slice into 4 slightly wedge-shaped fingers. Cut a round of bread to fit the bottom of an ovenproof pudding basin, which should be first buttered and sprinkled with caster sugar.

Line the bowl with the fingers of bread, buttered side down. Mix half the cream and half the sherry with the apple. Set aside the best mint leaves for decorating, then chop the rest and add to the apple, together with a little lemon juice. Spoon into the bowl, cover with a bread lid and press down. Bake in a preheated oven at 180°C/350°F/Gas4 for 10 minutes. Remove from the oven and allow to rest while you make the sauce.

Heat the jam in a saucepan, add the rest of the sherry, a little water if necessary, and the rest of the cream. Turn the pudding out on to a plate, strain the sauce over it, or hand separately, and decorate with toasted almonds and mint leaves.

Apple and Almond Crumble | serves 6–8

900g (2lb) apples, peeled, cored and diced or sliced
4 cloves
unrefined sugar, to taste

For the crumble
175g (6oz) plain flour
150g (5oz) butter
115g (4oz) ground almonds
55–85g (2–3oz) light muscovado sugar or golden caster sugar (not dark sugar)
25–55g (1–2oz) flaked almonds

Simmer the apples in a little water for 10–15 minutes with the cloves, and sweeten to taste with sugar. Transfer the fruit to individual ramekins, removing the cloves.

To make the crumble, rub the butter and flour together and stir in the ground almonds and sugar, keeping the mixture loose. Spoon the crumble over the fruit, and scatter on the flaked almonds.

Bake in a preheated oven at 200°C/400°F/Gas6 for 15 minutes. Serve hot or warm, with a pouring custard or *crème anglaise* flavoured and coloured with saffron strands and a vanilla ice-cream made with mead as the sweetener. A little extra honey can be added if necessary.

Cheese and Apple Tart, West Country Style

serves 6–8

For the pastry
225g (8oz) plain flour
55g (2oz) ground almonds
pinch of salt
3 tablespoons ground golden granulated sugar, or icing sugar, sifted
150g (5oz) unsalted butter
1 free-range egg yolk, lightly beaten
iced water

For the filling
2 Bramley apples
175g (6oz) Sharpham or Somerset Brie cheese, not too ripe, rind removed
300ml (½ pint) single cream
2 free-range eggs
2–3 tablespoons Somerset cider brandy or Calvados
85–115g (3–4oz) golden caster or light muscovado sugar

To make the pastry, sift the dry ingredients together into a bowl. Rub in the butter lightly, and then add the egg yolk and enough water to bind. Gather the pastry into a ball. Cover, and refrigerate for 20 minutes. Roll out, and line a 23–25cm (9–10in) pie dish. Prick the pastry all over with a fork. Line with greaseproof paper, fill with baking beans, and bake blind in a preheated oven at 180°C/350°F/Gas 4 for 15–20 minutes.

To make the filling, peel, core and slice the apples, and slice the cheese. Arrange in the base of the parbaked pastry case. Beat the rest of the ingredients together, and pour over the apple and cheese. Bake for 30 minutes in a preheated oven at 200°C/400°F/Gas 6, then turn the oven down to 180°C/350°F/Gas 4 and bake for a further 15–20 minutes. Serve the tart hot or warm.

Apple and Pear Sorbets

Tropical fruit sorbets are fashionable, but one can tire of their insistent flavours and vivid colour. For the very best sorbets, apples are hard to beat. In their infinite variety they provide a whole palette of colours, textures and aromas, as well as sorbets for every season. Even if you cannot find the apples to serve a Cornish Aromatic, D'Arcy Spice, Melcombe Russet or Green Balsam sorbet, consider the perfumed sweetness of a Worcester Pearmain sorbet, or the dry nuttiness of an Egremont Russet. A Granny Smith makes a marvellously tart, mouth-tingling sorbet, and a really ripe flushed Golden Delicious, a mouthful of sweetness, but it is hard to beat a Bramley Seedling sorbet.

To prepare apples for sorbet, quarter and core them, then roughly chop, and put into a food processor or blender with a couple of tablespoons of water and a teaspoon or two of lemon juice to prevent discolouring. I like to keep a little of the peel on for the flecked effect it gives. Blend to a purée, then mix with the syrup as described on page 245. I find it worthwhile keeping a bottle of syrup on hand for making sorbets. It is a sad fact that the smoothest-textured sorbets require the most sugar.

I prefer to use raw apples, but interesting variations can be created with different apples cooked into a purée and then flavoured with cinnamon, cloves or cardamom. For another version, simply freeze cider into a sorbet or a coarser granita.

If you have picked lots of apples or pears, it is worth freezing them for making instant sorbets. Peel, core and quarter the fruit, brush with lemon juice to prevent it from discolouring, and open-freeze it on a tray before putting into labelled bags. To make an instant sorbet, put the fruit pieces into a food processor with a little cold water (about 4 tablespoons per 450g (1lb) of fruit) and sugar syrup (see below) to taste. Switch on and process until smooth. Pile into glasses and serve immediately.

Sugar Syrup

1.2kg (2½lb) granulated sugar
600ml (1 pint) water

Dissolve the sugar in the water in a heavy pan over a low heat, bring to the boil and boil for 1 minute. Cool, bottle and refrigerate.

To make sorbet, dilute the syrup with equal quantities of water, and add fruit pulp in equal volume to the liquid used. Stir in the juice of ½ a lemon. Blend thoroughly and freeze, either in an ice-cream maker or sorbetière, according to the manufacturer's instructions. The mixture can also be frozen in a container in the freezer or ice-making part of the refrigerator. As the mixture freezes and crystals form, it will need to be stirred from time to time. To ensure a smooth sorbet, it is quite a good plan to give it its final stir in a food processor before putting it back into the freezer. Sorbets are best eaten within a few hours of being made.

Pear Sorbet | serves 10–12

Pears are much sweeter than apples, and you can make them into excellent sorbets.

1.5kg (3¼lb) pears
fresh ginger root
sugar
water

Peel, core and gently cook the pears, with just a little ginger for seasoning. Make a purée, and while hot add one part sugar to two parts water and four parts fruit purée. Freeze, and allow to ripen by removing from the freezer for 20 minutes or so before serving.

Vanilla Baked Apples and Pears | serves 4

2–3 bread rolls or saffron buns (see page 225), sliced to give 8 slices
115g (4oz) unsalted butter
4 vanilla pods
4 apples
4 pears
85–115g (3–4oz) light muscovado sugar
1 orange
1 lemon
several tablespoons Somerset apple brandy

Thickly butter the bread slices, and place them in a lightly buttered ovenproof dish. Cut the vanilla pods in half and split them lengthways. Spike the pieces of vanilla into the unpeeled, uncored fruit, using a skewer to make the holes if necessary.

Place a fruit on each slice of bread. Smear the rest of the butter over them, and sprinkle with the sugar. Pare the citrus fruit zest in spirals, arrange amongst the fruit, and squeeze on a little of the juices. Bake in a preheated oven at 175°C/325°F/Gas 3 for 50–60 minutes. Remove from the oven, pour on the brandy, and serve when just warm with clotted cream, crème fraiche or thick yoghurt.

Baked Plums

I have also made a similar dish to the above with plums, which I like very much. Allow 3–4 Victorias or Marjorie Seedlings per person. Cut in half lengthways, and remove the stones. Fill the hollows with a mixture of butter and sugar or almond paste, and pin the fruit together again with a sliver of vanilla pod. Arrange the fruit in half a hollowed-out bread roll or on a slice of bread brushed with melted butter, dot with a little more butter and sugar, and bake in a preheated oven at 180°C/ 350°F/Gas 4 for 30–40 minutes. Pour on a little plum liqueur or Mirabelle eau de vie before serving.

Pear Tarts with Liquorice Custard | serves 2

For the custard
300ml (½ pint) milk
55g (2oz) liquorice root (not the confectionery)
2 free-range egg yolks
85g (3oz) caster sugar
1 level tablespoon cornflour

225g (8oz) puff pastry
2 pears, peeled, cored and sliced
icing sugar

To make the custard, put the milk and liquorice root into a saucepan. Bring gently to the boil. In a bowl mix the egg yolks, sugar and cornflour, and pour on the scalded milk, stirring well. Pour back into the saucepan, and simmer gently for a couple of minutes, stirring gently. Remove from the heat, and allow to stand for at least an hour for the liquorice to infuse. Discard the liquorice root before using.

Roll out the pastry, and cut out 2 × 12.5cm (5in) rounds. Place on a baking sheet and bake in a preheated oven at 200°C/400°F/Gas 6 for 12–15 minutes. Remove from the oven. Arrange the pears on top, and sift with icing sugar. Place under a hot grill for a few minutes to caramelize the pears. Put the tarts on plates, and serve with the custard.

Note

Liquorice roots can be bought in some healthfood/wholefood shops and herbalists. If you prefer, make a coffee custard, replacing the liquorice roots with a tablespoon of coarsely ground coffee beans. The custard will need straining. Vanilla custard is also very good with pears, as is custard perfumed with a spoonful or two of *eau de vie de poire*, fragrant pear spirit from Alsace.

Pears in Blackcurrant Liqueur | serves 6

The fruit farms in the West Country produce some excellent fruit liqueurs, and I use the blackcurrant one with pears.

6 Conference or firm Williams pears
6 cloves
1 cinnamon stick
grating of nutmeg
2–3 slices of orange
150ml (¼ pint) sweet white wine
100ml (3½ fl oz) blackcurrant liqueur

Peel the pears carefully, leaving the stalks on if possible. Put all the ingredients into a large heavy saucepan, sticking a clove in the base of each pear. Bring to the boil, then simmer gently until the pears are tender.

Transfer the pears to large wine glasses or serving dishes. Strain the cooking juices, and boil down to a syrup. Pour over the pears. This is very good with crème fraiche or thick plain yoghurt.

Vermouth Blackcurrant

On the subject of liqueurs, I recommend this lovely refreshing aperitif.

measure of blackcurrant liqueur
measure of dry vermouth
sparkling mineral water

Combine the fruit liqueur and vermouth, and top up with mineral water.

Rosehip and Raspberry Pie | serves 4–6

This is a pie for early autumn, when the rose petals have dropped. It usually coincides with a second crop of raspberries.

350g (12oz) shortcrust pastry
225g (8oz) rosehips, the larger the better
225g (8oz) raspberries
55–85g (2–3oz) golden caster sugar
2 tablespoons lemon juice
1 tablespoon cornflour
pinch of ground mace
freshly grated nutmeg
200ml (⅓ pint) double or whipping cream
2 free-range egg yolks

Line a 25cm (10in) pie dish with half the pastry, and put the rest to one side for the lid. Slit the rosehips, and with a pointed spoon, remove the seeds. Rinse, drain and simmer with a little extra water until tender. Drain once more, and allow to cool. Mix them with the raspberries and sugar. Stir the lemon juice, cornflour and spices together, and mix into the fruit. Spoon the fruit into the lined pie dish. Roll out a lid, place on top and seal the edges. Make a small hole in the lid.

Bake in a preheated oven at 180°C/350°F/Gas4 for about 45 minutes. Remove the pie from the oven 10–15 minutes before it is ready, and into the hole pour the cream and egg yolks, beaten together. Return the pie to the oven to finish baking.

Note

For a lighter version of this recipe, which makes it into more of a tart, leave out the custard and top with a lattice of pastry rather than a crust. It will require about 280g (10 oz) pastry in all.

Apple and Elderflower Fritters | serves 4

200g (7oz) plain flour
pinch of salt
2 teaspoons fast-action easy-blend dried yeast granules
1 free-range egg
150ml (¼ pint) warm milk
1 apple, peeled and finely diced
grated zest of 1 lemon
1–2 tablespoons lemon juice
55–85g (2–3oz) elderflowers, stripped from their stalks
oil for frying

For serving
icing sugar

Mix the dry ingredients in a bowl, then beat in the egg and milk until you have a smooth, thick batter. Stir in the apple, lemon zest and juice, and finally fold in the elderflowers.

Heat the oil in a deep-fryer to 180°C (350°F), and fry the fitters one at a time, scooping the batter mixture off a dessertspoon, until golden-brown. Drain on paper towels, and serve hot, dusted with icing sugar.

Gooseberry and Almond Crumble | serves 4–6

about 1kg (generous 2lb) gooseberries, topped and tailed
vanilla pod
unrefined sugar, to taste

For the crumble
115g (4oz) plain flour
85g (3oz) butter
55g (2oz) ground almonds
55–85g (2–3oz) light muscovado sugar
25g (1oz) flaked almonds

Simmer the gooseberries with the vanilla in a little water for 10–15 minutes, and sweeten to taste. Transfer the fruit to individual ramekins, removing the vanilla.

To make the crumble, rub the butter and flour together, and stir in the ground almonds and sugar, keeping the mixture loose.

Spoon the crumble over the fruit, and scatter on the flaked almonds. Bake in a preheated oven at 200°C/400°F/Gas6 for 15 minutes. Serve hot or warm, with a custard or *crème anglaise* sweetened with elderflower syrup.

Summer Pudding | serves 6–8, × 2

I know that strawberries are not traditionally correct in a summer pudding, but I have included a few because they are so readily available in summer in the West Country. I recommend making 2 because this pudding freezes so well.

For each pudding
some, or all, of the following, to about 675g (1½lb) weight. There should be a good proportion of redcurrants and raspberries, for both flavour and their setting property:
- *raspberries*
- *redcurrants*
- *loganberries*
- *white-currants*
- *strawberries*

85–115g (3–4oz) sugar
slices of white bread, crusts removed

Rinse and drain the fruit, topping, tailing and hulling where necessary. Put into a saucepan, and sprinkle over the sugar. Set over a low heat until the juices run and the sugar dissolves.

Add up to 4 tablespoons of water to encourage the juice to run. Check for sweetness.

Remove from the heat. Start lining the pudding basin with bread. I find this works best if you cut square slices into 2 wedge-shaped pieces, and place these, narrow end down, in the basin, having first dipped the pieces of bread in the fruit juice. Continue overlapping the slices tightly until the basin is fully lined.

Cut a small circle of bread to fit the bottom. Pour in the fruit to fill the basin. The bread will quickly absorb the juice: reserve a few tablespoons of it. Fit slices of bread over the top so that the fruit is completely covered. Cover with a saucer, and place a weight on top to pack the whole thing as tightly as possible. Refrigerate.

To serve, unmould on to a plate, and surround with the reserved juice. Serve with clotted cream, crème fraiche, ricotta or fromage blanc, if you like.

To freeze one of the puddings, having weighted it down for a day, turn it out, then transfer it to a lidded plastic Christmas pudding container. Or, indeed, construct the pudding in the first place in one of these very useful containers. Cover, wrap in clingfilm and freeze. Freeze the extra juice separately. To serve, thaw out and allow to come to room temperature.

Wild Fruit Table Jelly | serves 8–10

If you are making jellies and preserves, you can make a very glamorous ending to a meal if you save some of the juice extracted and turn it into a table jelly, especially effective if you have an old-fashioned jelly mould. What else you add to the extract depends a little on its composition. Rowanberries have a sophisticated, smoky flavour, which is enhanced by the addition of Madeira. Apple brandy or cider can be used with crab apples, port with elderberries, red wine with blackberries, but there are no hard and fast rules; use whatever appeals. You will need plenty of sugar or syrup, as the fruit extract will be sour, if not bitter.

8 leaves of gelatine or 8 teaspoons powdered gelatine
300ml (½ pint) water
600ml (1 pint) extracted fruit juice
juice of 1 lemon
300ml (½ pint) wine, or cider, or 150ml (¼ pint) fortified wine mixed with 150ml (¼ pint) water or fruit juice
sugar, to taste

Soak the gelatine in half the water until softened, then add the rest of the water. Heat gently without boiling and stir until dissolved. Add it to the fruit extract and lemon juice. Heat the wine, cider or diluted fortified wine, and boil for 2–3 minutes to evaporate the alcohol. Stir into the fruit liquid, and then, while still warm, stir in enough sugar to sweeten.

Pour the liquid into a wetted jelly mould, and when cool, refrigerate for several hours, ideally overnight, until set. Turn out, and decorate as you wish.

Eighteenth-century English Trifle | serves 10

For the sponge
4 free-range eggs, separated
120g (generous 4oz) icing sugar
120g (generous 4oz) self-raising flour, sifted

For the custard
1 vanilla pod
400ml (14fl oz) milk
300ml (½ pint) single cream
8 free-range egg yolks
85g (3oz) caster sugar

To finish
apricot glaze, or redcurrant jelly
12 amaretti biscuits
150ml (¼ pint) cream sherry, such as Valdespino Cream or Harveys Bristol Cream

For the topping
500ml (18fl oz) whipping cream
toasted flaked almonds

To make the sponge, whisk the egg yolks over hot water with half the sugar until pale and thick enough to leave a ribbon. Whisk the egg whites, adding the remaining sugar.

Fold the flour into the egg yolk mixture, and fold the two mixtures carefully together. Spread in a prepared Swiss roll tray. Bake in a preheated oven at 180°C/350°F/Gas4 for 10–12 minutes.

Turn the sponge out. Trim off the crisp edges. Roll up loosely from one long end.

Use the custard ingredients to make up into a thick custard in the usual way. Infuse the vanilla pod in the milk and cream as you scald it in a saucepan. Scrape the vanilla seeds into the custard and allow to cool. Beat the egg yolks with the sugar and pour on the infused milk and cream. Return the mixture to the saucepan and cook very gently until it just coats the back of a spoon, but do not let it boil or the eggs will curdle.

Unroll the sponge, spread with the glaze or jelly; roll up again and slice it. Line the bottom of a glass bowl with the sponge slices. Place the amaretti on top, and moisten with the sherry.

Spoon on the custard, and chill to set slightly. Whip the cream until firm and spread on top. Arrange the flaked almonds round the edge and in a daisy pattern on top.

West Country Syllabub | serves 6–8

Syllabub is another old-fashioned English dessert, and where better to make it than the West Country, with its excellent cream? In some parts of the country, syllabub is made with ale. I prefer it with wine, but a medium cider also does the trick. Match cider with cider brandy or Calvados, and wine with cognac.

75ml (⅛ pint) Somerset cider brandy, Calvados or cognac
¼ nutmeg, grated
115–150g (4–5oz) golden caster sugar
300ml (½ pint) cider or sweet white wine
850ml (1½ pints) double cream

Infuse the brandy with nutmeg and sugar, and leave overnight. Stir in the cider or wine. In a large bowl, whip the cream, and then gradually incorporate the liquid. Serve in chilled glasses.

Lavender Ice cream | serves 8

Note that this recipe uses uncooked eggs.

175g (6oz) granulated sugar
15g (½oz) fresh lavender buds, plus extra heads for decoration
300ml (½ pint) full-cream milk
300ml (½ pint) single cream, or 225g (8oz) crème fraiche
6 free-range egg yolks

In a clean coffee grinder, or with a mortar and pestle, grind 150g (5oz) of the sugar and the lavender flowers until thoroughly blended. Stir into the milk, and bring to the boil. Beat the cream and egg yolks together in a bowl, and pour the lavender-flavoured milk into it, stirring all the time.

Return the mixture to the saucepan, and cook very gently until it just coats the back of a spoon, but do not let it boil or the eggs will curdle. Allow to cool, then freeze, either in a machine or in the freezer.

Crystallize the lavender flowers by dipping in water, rolling in the remaining sugar and placing them on a piece of paper to dry. Scoop out the ice cream, and decorate with crystallized lavender.

A West Country Tea

Here are some of my favourite teatime recipes for those few occasions when we can enjoy the luxury of this somewhat labour-intensive meal. In fact, we rarely had the chance to do this at the Mill, but I do remember a pair of glorious June afternoons when we had several visitors coming to do interviews and take photographs. It was the excuse I needed to bake batches of scones, and make some strawberry jelly with the fruit I had bought from roadside stalls once we reached Cornwall. And with the scones and jam I served clotted cream, in a true West Country cream tea, which is one of the glories of the English culinary repertoire, quite unique and a tradition still preserved in this part of the country.

Asparagus and Chicken Sandwiches | serves 2–4

In the West Country, fresh crab is my favourite sandwich filling, but when I can get English asparagus, this is a close second, especially if the chicken is left over from a Swaddles Farm roasted organic chicken.

175g (6oz) cooked chicken
55g (2oz) softened butter or polyunsaturated margarine
4–5 tablespoons chicken gravy
2–3 cooked garlic cloves (optional)
a few sprigs of fresh parsley or chives
grated lemon zest
1 teaspoon lemon juice
white pepper
8–10 asparagus stalks, cooked

Chop the chicken and mix it, by hand or in a food processor, with the butter or margarine, gravy, garlic, herbs, lemon zest and juice, and pepper. When smooth, chill the mixture a little to firm it up, if necessary. Spread on bread or muffins, and cut the asparagus stalks to fit. Butter the second slice of bread or muffin-half and place on top.

For an extra-luxurious version, I spread a spoonful of leftover sauce mousseline on top of the asparagus.

Cucumber Sandwiches

Take 3 cucumbers, and shave off the thinnest layer of skin with a swivel-blade potato peeler. Halve the cucumbers lengthways, and discard the watery core of seeds. Thinly slice the halved cucumbers, put into a colander with a good sprinkling of salt, and leave to degorge for an hour or so. Rinse thoroughly, drain, and dry by rolling and wringing in a clean tea-towel. The cucumber will keep in the refrigerator for 2–3 days, and makes an excellent, crisp filling for thin brown or white bread sandwiches – the perfect cucumber sandwich, in fact.

More fillings for thin sandwiches

I like to use smoked salmon, creamed crab, using the soft brown crabmeat, and salmon paste, which I make by mixing cooked salmon, soft butter, spices and seasoning. The prepared cucumber is also very good combined with cream cheese and chives.

Thick sandwiches

For a more substantial tea, I find that English muffins make excellent sandwiches. Warm them through, split them, remove a little of the inside crumb, and choose from among the following fillings:

Crabmeat and asparagus: White crabmeat mixed with mayonnaise and cooked asparagus tips.

Avocado and asparagus: For vegetarians, combine diced avocado, asparagus tips, chopped spring onions and mayonnaise, flavoured with a little orange juice and grated orange zest.

BLT: A muffin is the perfect vehicle for the classic bacon, lettuce and tomato sandwich, with a slick of mayonnaise.

Chicken liver: Fry some trimmed rashers of bacon until crisp, then some sliced mushrooms and chicken liver. Roughly squash or mash together the mushrooms and chicken liver, crumble the bacon and fill the muffin with this mixture, together with some cress, shredded lettuce or other greenery. Serve warm or cold.

Tuna fish or salmon salad: Flake the cooked fish, and mix with the chopped celery, spring onions, a little lemon juice and grated lemon zest and mayonnaise.

Prawn, mint, chilli and cucumber: Chop cooked prawns and mint, and mix with prepared cucumber, thick plain yoghurt and a little finely chopped chilli.

Smoked trout, or mackerel: Mash the smoked fish roughly with some horseradish, and mix with freshly ground pepper and soured cream. Good with prepared cucumber or lettuce hearts.

Raspberry Sandwiches

Here is a lovely idea for a summer teatime treat, to follow your savoury finger sandwiches. Instead of butter, the bread can be spread with clotted cream.

Take generously buttered slices of good bread and some ripe raspberries, rolled in caster sugar. Fork the raspberries to a pulp, spread on the bread and sandwich together. Mulberries are equally fine used in this way.

Scones | makes about 8

After the sandwiches, something warm, but rather plain, is always very appealing – scones, griddle cakes or crumpets, for preference. Scones are so quick and easy to make that it is a pity to buy them. I usually only want to make 8–10 at a time, and for this quantity, it is not worth getting out the food processor. In any case, quick, light, cool hands make a much better scone dough than a machine.

Spices, dried fruit and mixed peel are possible additions, but I like my scones absolutely plain and barely sweet. Clotted cream is the ideal topping, or unsalted butter. It is a matter of personal taste, but I do not like double cream, whipped cream, or crème fraiche as substitutes. Home-made jam or jelly goes on before, or after; I am not dogmatic about that. And sometimes lemon curd is just the right thing on scones, unless you want to keep it to sandwich a plain Victoria sponge. On the whole, I favour that plan, with fruit jelly or strawberry jam on the scones.

280g (10oz) plain flour
4 scant teaspoons baking powder
pinch of salt
2 teaspoons caster sugar
85g (3oz) unsalted butter, chilled and diced
iced water mixed with plain yoghurt
free-range egg beaten with a little milk, to glaze

Sift the dry ingredients together into a large bowl and rub in the butter. With a knife, and a light hand, stir in just enough of the water and yoghurt mixture to bind the dough. Turn it out on to a floured work top and knead and pat lightly to make a smooth round. Cut out the scones and place together on a non-stick baking sheet.

Brush with an egg and milk glaze, if you wish, and bake in a preheated oven at 180°C/350°F/Gas4 for about 15 minutes or so, until well risen and golden-brown. Transfer to a wire rack to cool.

West Country Ginger Biscuits | makes 2 dozen

200g (7oz) plain flour
2 teaspoons ground ginger
½ teaspoon ground mixed spice
pinch of saffron strands, rubbed to a powder
pinch of salt
175g (6oz) unsalted butter, softened
175g (6oz) golden caster sugar or light muscovado sugar

Sift the dry ingredients together into a large bowl. Cream the butter and sugar until pale and fluffy. Stir the two together, mixing thoroughly. Form the mixture into 24 balls. Place on greased or silicone paper-lined baking trays, and press down with the base of a glass, a decorative one if you wish.

Bake in a preheated oven at 180°C/350°F/Gas4 for 8–10 minutes until golden-brown. Transfer to a wire rack to cool.

New Elizabethan Biscuits | makes about 3 dozen

Saffron and rosewater, which you can buy from chemists and good food shops, were popular as flavourings in Elizabethan times, both in sweet and savoury dishes, and I have used them in my biscuit recipe, combining them with other flavours used at that period. These biscuits, which I originally developed for a feature on Elizabethan food, are lovely served with fruit fools and junkets, as well as for afternoon tea.

225g (8oz) unsalted butter at room temperature
225g (8oz) caster sugar
1 free-range egg
75ml (⅛ pint) full-cream milk infused with a good pinch of saffron strands
2–3 teaspoons rosewater
55g (2oz) dried apricots, finely chopped
pinch of ground cardamom
pinch of ground cinnamon
150g (5oz) plain flour
25g (1oz) ground rice
55g (2oz) ground almonds

Cream the butter and sugar until pale and fluffy. Beat in the egg, and then add the milk, rosewater, apricots and spices. Mix in the dry ingredients until you have a stiff dough. Roll out on to a floured top, and cut into 4cm (1½in) rounds. Place on a baking sheet, and chill for 15–20 minutes in the refrigerator.

Bake in a preheated oven at 170°C/325°F/Gas3 for about 30 minutes. Transfer to a wire rack to cool.

Somerset Brandy Snaps | makes 20

55g (2oz) unsalted butter
55g (2oz) caster sugar or light muscovado sugar
2 tablespoons golden syrup
55g (2oz) plain flour, sifted
good pinch of ground ginger
1 tablespoon Somerset cider brandy
2 teaspoons grated lemon zest

Grease the narrow handles of wooden spoons to shape the brandy snaps. Heat the butter, sugar and golden syrup in a small heavy saucepan until the butter has melted. Remove from the heat, and mix in the rest of the ingredients. Line a baking sheet with silicone paper, and drop very small spoonfuls of the mixture, well spaced, on to the sheet. Bake in a preheated oven at 180°C/350°F/Gas4 for 8–10 minutes, until golden brown and lacy.

Remove from the oven, leave for a minute or two to firm up, lift off the paper, and while still warm and pliable shape round the greased wooden handles. When set, gently remove, and cool on wire racks.

Note

I like brandy snaps quite plain like this, but you can pipe whipped cream into them, or serve them with clotted cream.

Tipsy Fruit Cake

225g (8oz) unsalted butter
280g (10oz) dark muscovado sugar or molasses
4 free-range eggs, lightly beaten
450g (1lb) self-raising flour
pinch of salt
4 tablespoons orange or lemon marmalade
100g (3½oz) each chopped walnuts, raisins and chopped mixed peel, undyed
1 teaspoon pure vanilla essence
6 tablespoons rum, brandy or cider brandy
milk

Cream the butter and sugar until light and fluffy. Beat in the eggs and flour alternately. Stir in the rest of the ingredients, except for half the spirit, and add enough milk to give the mixture a soft dropping consistency. Grease and line a loaf tin, and spoon in the mixture.

Smooth the top, and bake in a preheated oven at 150°C/300°F/Gas 3 for 2 hours. Allow to cool in the tin. Turn out and pour the remaining spirit over the cake, having pierced holes in it with a skewer.

Cover the cake with kitchen foil, and allow to stand in a cool place until the spirit is absorbed. Then wrap the cake in greaseproof paper and foil. It will keep for several weeks.

Ginger Cake

Cakes and biscuits flavoured with ginger have been popular in England since the Middle Ages.

450g (1lb) plain flour
1 tablespoon ground ginger
1 tablespoon baking powder
1 teaspoon salt
1 teaspoon bicarbonate of soda
175g (6oz) black treacle
175g (6oz) golden syrup
225g (8oz) light or dark muscovado sugar
175g (6oz) unsalted butter
300ml (½ pint) semi-skimmed milk
2 size 3 free-range eggs
2–3 teaspoons finely chopped preserved ginger, or peeled and grated fresh ginger root

Sift the dry ingredients together into a large bowl. Warm the treacle, golden syrup, sugar and butter together in a saucepan until the butter has melted, then stir into the dry ingredients. Beat in the milk, eggs and ginger.

Mix thoroughly, and pour the batter into a greased and lined cake tin, about 25cm (10 in) square and 4cm (1½in) deep. Bake in a preheated oven at 180°C/350°F/Gas 4 for about 1½ hours until well risen and just firm to the touch in the centre. Leave to cool in the tin for 15 minutes or so, then turn out and cool on a wire rack.

Wrap the cake in kitchen foil, still in its greaseproof paper lining, and store for about a week to allow the flavours to develop. Ginger cakes of all kinds really do need keeping for a few days; both texture and flavour will be improved.

Note

To make a style of cake more like parkin, use about 55g (2oz) less fat, 100g (3½oz) less sugar, and replace half the flour with oatmeal or oatflakes. This slightly drier mixture will bake in less time than the ginger cake.

With so many types of unrefined sugar now available, ginger cake is a good recipe to experiment with. If you like a very dark, richly flavoured cake, use dark muscovado or molasses sugar; for a paler colour and lighter flavour, use demerara, light muscovado, or even unrefined caster sugar. It is important to use the syrup and treacle, however, since this is what gives the cake its characteristic heaviness and stickiness.

Victoria Sponge

175g (6oz) unsalted butter
175g (6oz) golden caster sugar
3 large free-range eggs
175g (6oz) self-raising flour, sifted

For the filling
raspberry jam, with buttercream or clotted cream, or lemon curd

To finish
icing sugar

Cream the butter and sugar thoroughly until pale, light and fluffy. Beat the eggs, and gradually beat them, a little at a time, into the creamed mixture. Once the eggs have been incorporated, gently fold in the flour.

Spoon the batter into 2 × 20 cm (8 in) greased and floured sandwich tins and smooth the tops. Bake in a preheated oven at 180°C/350°F/Gas 4 for 20–25 minutes.

Allow to cool in the tins for a few minutes, then ease the sponges out on to wire racks to cool.

To serve, sandwich with raspberry jam and buttercream or clotted cream, if you wish, or with lemon curd. Sift icing sugar over the top.

Lemon Barley Water | makes about 1.25 litres (2 pints)

Tea in the garden on a summer afternoon might well lend itself to homely, refreshing cold drinks rather than, or perhaps as well as, the traditional cuppa.

2 unsprayed lemons
85g (3oz) pearl barley
1.25 litres (2 pints) water
sugar or sugar syrup (see page 245), to taste

With a potato peeler, pare off the lemon zest, and put it into a saucepan with the pearl barley and half the water. Squeeze the lemons and reserve the juice. Pull out the pulp from the lemon halves and add to the pan.

Bring to the boil, then simmer for 30–40 minutes. Remove from the heat, mash the pulp, and leave to stand for an hour or so. Scoop out a tablespoon or so of barley, and put it into a large jug. Sieve the cooked pulp into it, add the squeezed juice and the rest of the water, and sweeten to taste. Cover and refrigerate. This is even better the day after it is made.

Iced Ginger Tea | makes 1.25 litres (2 pints), to be diluted

5cm (2in) piece of fresh ginger root
1 tablespoon Ceylon or Darjeeling tea
1.25 litres (2 pints) boiling water
sugar or sugar syrup, to taste
still or sparkling mineral water
fresh orange slices or wedges
mint leaves

Peel and slice the ginger, and put it into a jug. Put the tea into another jug or teapot, and pour boiling water into each. Leave to steep for 5 minutes, then strain both into one large glass jug. Stir in sugar or syrup.

Allow to cool, then refrigerate. When very cold, dilute with water, decorate with orange and mint and serve. This will also do very well, as will the Lemon Barley Water, in a thermos jug.

Cheese, Preserves and Other Good Things

Cheese

Sharpham Estate, near Totnes, gently hugs the sloping meadows above the River Dart, which here curves round to embrace not only pastures for grazing the Jersey cows from whose milk Debbie Mumford makes the rich, creamy Sharpham cheese, but vineyards. Vines thrive in the gentle, nurturing microclimate, as do all good vineyards near great rivers, which keeps away that scourge of the vine, frost. With his grapes Mark Sharman makes very fine wines, especially from the Madeleine Angevine grape. He also plants, in his 'back garden', merlot and cabernet sauvignon, the grapes used in the classic wines of Bordeaux. His Beenleigh 1990 is a revelation: elegant, with a fine structure and good length, supple, delightful on the nose as well as to the eye and on the palate. After tasting this and his Estate Selection, and the Estate Reserve, which is partially aged in new oak, my long-held views about English wine were changed. This was not just very good 'for an English wine', it was very good. Lovely with fish and poultry dishes, this white wine also proves a fine companion to the estate's cheese, the soft, white Sharpham, a bloomy, Coulommiers-type cheese, with a rich, buttery colour, slightly piquant flavour and creamy texture.

Making cheese – making real cheese – is hard work. It is an agricultural product, born of the soil, the pasture and the climate, as well as the skill of the cheese-maker and the breed of dairy cow, goat or sheep. Once described as 'milk's leap to immortality', cheese-making goes back thousands of years to the first livestock farmers, who almost certainly discovered the process by accident.

Although cheese-making has become more sophisticated since its simple beginnings, the process remains essentially the same in all cheese-making areas of the world. I have visited cheese-makers in France, Switzerland and Italy, and the moist, warm, appetizing smell in the Caseficio San Giovanni in the heart of Italy's Modenese countryside, or in La Ferme de Frience high up in the Swiss Alps near Villars, is not unlike that of the cheese dairy at Sharpham Barton in Devon, just down the lane from the Sharpham Estate, where Robin Congdon makes his range of fine West Country cheeses, using milk from local farmers who raise sheep, goats and cows on the rich Devon pasture.

In the early sixteenth century Totnes was one of the twelve richest towns in England; handsome houses belonging to the tin and wool merchants lined the main street. Through it flows the wide River Dart. Butter Walk and Poultry Walk are relics of the town's agricultural history. Perhaps there should now be a street named Cheese Walk. But Ticklemore Street is its name, and in it you will find the Ticklemore Cheese Shop, owned and run by Sari Cooper, Robin Congdon's partner, who sells his cheeses as well as many other West Country cheeses.

More than anything else I was impressed by Sari's descriptions of these marvellous English cheeses – blue cheeses, goat's cheeses, soft cheeses – and not once did she compare them to, for example, Roquefort or Gorgonzola. As Sari pointed out, these are unique cheeses, with their own distinctive flavour and texture, and not made to resemble other cheeses.

We also met a 'second-generation' cheese-maker in the person of Jeremy Frankpitt. He bought the recipe and name of Devon Garland when its originator, Hilary Charnleigh, retired. He makes the cheese with unpasteurized milk from his brother Michael's herd of Friesian cows, in the well-planned cheese dairy designed by a third brother, Marcus Frankpitt, an engineer. As well as Devon Garland, Jeremy Frankpitt also makes Knightswood to his own recipe, a very agreeable cheese with a good, sharp, mouth-filling tang, which softens to a mellow creaminess as the cheese matures. In truth, I prefer cheeses without any additives, and like the Knightswood better than the Devon Garland.

The cheese-makers I have met over the years in Britain and abroad are, without exception, one of the most skilled, dedicated, careful and enthusiastic bands of people you could hope to meet. And they produce, individually, some of the great glories of our table.

It has been a long time since I have looked to the continent for my cheeses, as the British Isles provides more than enough to put together a world-class cheeseboard. I would be hard put, in fact, to select my ideal cheeseboard. One thing I do know: it would consist of no more than five cheeses, including a blue cheese, a soft bloomy cheese, perhaps a washed-rind cheese, a hard cheese and a goat's cheese. And I would take them out of the refrigerator a couple of hours before serving them.

My ideal West Country cheeseboard has a mixture of types

and textures, which is important. My hard cheese would probably be a Ticklemore Goat and, as an alternative, because not everyone likes goat's cheese, I would add a Keen's or Montgomery Cheddar. The blue would be one of Robin Congdon's, either his Beenleigh Blue ewe's milk, or his Harbourne goat's cheese. The soft white rind cheese might be the Sharpham or the Somerset Brie. Mennallack, Cornish Yarg, Devon Garland, Knightswood, Coleford, Wootton, Ladywell, Capricon, Loddiswell, Vulscombe, Dorset Blue Vinney, Wheatland, Ashprington, Elmhirst, Smythyn, Curworthy, Belston and Devon Oke are other West Country cheeses to look out for.

Medal-winning cheeses are more and more widely available now. If they are not in your locality, demand them. Try some new ones too. Each time you buy an old favourite, also buy one you have never tried before. Staff in cheese shops, delicatessens and at supermarket counters will be pleased to offer you a taste.

A cheeseboard is the most obvious way to show off these lovely cheeses, but not the only way. I have been experimenting with different fruit and cheese pairings, which I recommend to you.

An autumn dessert platter

In September, we can enjoy sweet ripe English plums and fragrant muscat grapes from Italy. I like to serve these luscious fruits with Kentish cobnuts and the first of the wet walnuts from Grenoble. A soft white rind cheese, such as Somerset Brie or Sharpham, is an excellent partner.

The perfect pair

A ripe English pear, mellow and juicy, will go well with a hard cheese, and I would choose amongst Ticklemore Goat, Keen's Cheddar, and Menallack, a lovely farmhouse cheese from Cornwall.

'An apple pie without cheese is like a kiss without a squeeze'

A crisp, buttery, flaky crust, enclosing melting slices of Bramley apple, seasoned with a little unrefined sugar and unsalted butter, perhaps a hint of cinnamon, nutmeg or clove, but not all three at once, served warm or at room temperature, deserves a fine farmhouse cheese. Try it with Cornish Yarg.

Curious flavours

Washed-rind cheeses with their penetrating, rude, earthy, farmyardy aromas and piquant flavour deserve a partner of equal sophistication. Indeed, Edward Bunyard in the *Epicure's Companion* described washed-rind cheeses as being 'the abyss of decadence'. Medlars perhaps when they are fully ripe or 'bletted', later in the season, or a translucent, garnet-coloured poached quince in syrup would go well. The flavours of both will linger and linger.

Autumn blues

Made in the spring and summer and at their best in autumn and winter, our lovely blue cheeses made from goat's or ewe's milk have a fine balance of acidity, salt, sweetness, creaminess and crumbliness and subtle layers of tastes and after-tastes. They are perfect with a fine, crisp, fragrant Cox's Orange Pippin.

Cooking with cheese

When your fine West Country cheeseboard reaches the stage of more rind and crumbs than cheese, you may be able to rescue enough for cooking, for it would be a pity to waste even a scrap. When I had English cheeses sent to Bangkok for my dinner menus while cooking at the Dusit Thani hotel, the cost of transporting them was exceedingly high, about £22 per kilo, and this was several years ago. Such cheeses not being available through local importers, I was under instruction from chef Jacques Lafargue to use every scrap if I did not want his food costs to go through the roof.

Cheese scones, cheese straws and cheese tartlets made several appearances on my menu, and for the lunchtime buffet, I served Glamorgan sausages.

At home, when I have pieces of leftover cheese, I like to make individual soufflés to serve as a starter or in place of the cheese course, variations on the rarebit or rabbit as a quick lunch or supper dish, or combinations of cheese and vegetables in rather nice velvety, smooth soups.

Hard cheeses can be shaved over carpaccio, pasta and risotto, and can be grilled on radicchio leaves, or grated and pounded with nuts and herbs for a 'pesto' which has little to do with basil, except by association, and everything to do with mortar and pestle.

Leftovers of fresh goat's cheese and ewe's milk cheese, and the younger blue cheeses, can be turned into elegant little mousses or creams to be served as starters with, perhaps, a cucumber salad, or instead of the cheese course with fruit. They are also excellent in sauces for vegetables, or simply crumbled and stirred into freshly cooked pasta.

A Seasonal 'Pesto' | makes 400g (14oz)

55g (2oz) parsley, or a mixture of parsley and basil or chervil
115g (4oz) grated hard goat's or sheep's cheese, or Cheddar
115g (4oz) shelled fresh cobnuts, or walnuts
115g (4oz) unsalted butter, slightly softened

Remove the thick stems from the parsley, which should be dry, and roughly chop in a food processor. Add the rest of the ingredients, and blend until the mixture reaches the texture you prefer. Alternatively, and authentically, pound the nuts, and blend in the cheese and butter and very finely chopped herbs. You can add a touch of freshly grated nutmeg and/or freshly ground black pepper, if you like. Store in a jar or small jars. Without garlic to go rancid, this will keep as long as you would keep butter. It is very good indeed with a baked potato or on vegetables.

Celery and Blue Cheese | serves 4–6

1–2 heads of crisp celery
150g (5oz) West Country blue cheese
55g (2oz) rendered duck fat or unsalted butter
3 tablespoons crème fraiche
pinch of powdered saffron
115g (4oz) smoked streaky bacon, diced and fried until crisp

Using the inner, crisper stalks only (the outer stalks can be saved for soup), cut the celery into 7.5 cm (3 in) lengths. Cream the cheese and duck fat or butter, then mix in the crème fraiche, saffron and bacon pieces. Spoon or pipe into the celery stalks, and serve as an appetizer with drinks or as the cheese-savoury course. For a vegetarian version, unsalted butter can replace the duck fat and chopped stoned black olives the bacon.

Cheese Toasts

Hot savoury toasts are very good when made with blue cheese, and like stuffed celery, can play a number of parts – snack, savoury or hors d'oeuvre. These are called *diablotins* in the southwestern part of France where Roquefort is used, and the authentic Occitan version uses rendered goose or duck fat, as in the recipe above, for which butter can be substituted. Shell some fresh walnuts, and if you have the patience, skin them. Chop them very fine, and mix them with double the amount of blue cheese. Season with pepper. Melt the fat, and brush slices of bread on both sides, preferably coarse country bread, cut about 1cm (½in) thick. Bake in the oven until crisp and hot, spread with the nut and cheese mixture and serve immediately.

Cheese Rissoles | makes 12

280g (10oz) fresh breadcrumbs
225g (8oz) hard cheese, grated
1 leek, or 4 spring onions, trimmed and finely chopped
1 tablespoon chopped fresh chives
1 tablespoon chopped fresh parsley
1 teaspoon mustard powder
sea salt and freshly ground black pepper
freshly grated nutmeg
2 free-range eggs and 1 egg white
milk
flour or breadcrumbs for coating
25g (1oz) butter
1 tablespoon olive oil

Mix together the breadcrumbs, cheese, leek or onion, herbs and seasoning. Mix 1 whole egg and an egg yolk into the mixture and as much milk as is needed to bind it together. Whisk the egg whites to a froth on a plate, and put the flour or breadcrumbs in another. Divide the mixture into 12 equal portions, and roll them on a floured board into sausage shapes. Roll each one in the egg white and then in the flour or breadcrumbs. Heat the butter and oil in a frying pan, and fry for about 10 minutes until golden-brown. Serve hot, warm or cold. They are good with homemade tomato sauce, chutney or pickles.

Roasted Asparagus and Goat's Cheese Tart

serves 6

225g (8oz) shortcrust pastry
450g (1lb) fresh green English asparagus
olive oil or butter
coarse sea salt
225g (8oz) fresh goat's cheese
115g (4oz) curd cheese

Roll out the pastry, and line a loose-bottomed flan dish. Prick the base all over with a fork. Cover with greaseproof paper, fill with pasta or baking beans, and bake blind in a preheated oven at 200°C/400°F/Gas6 for 30 minutes. Allow to cool.

While the pastry is baking, cook the asparagus. Trim down to the tender part, roll them in the olive oil or melted butter, and place on a baking sheet. Roast until tender. Remove from the oven, and cool. Sprinkle with salt. (The asparagus can also be fried or cooked on a cast-iron griddle.) Beat the two cheeses together until smooth, and spread in the pastry case. Arrange the asparagus on top, and serve.

West Country Rarebit | serves 1

3 tablespoons scrumpy or dry cider
1 small apple, peeled and grated
85g (3oz) West Country cheese, such as Devon Garland, Cornish Yarg, Somerset Cheddar, or Dorset Blue, diced or grated
1 thick slice of bread, toasted on one side, buttered on the other, and spread with a little mustard

Put the cider and apple into a saucepan, and heat gently. Stir in the cheese, and when melted, spoon over the bread, buttered side up, which you have placed in an ovenproof dish.

Finish off under the grill, or in the top of a hot oven, until the top is bubbling and golden-brown. You can also make several of these, placing the toast in a large ovenproof dish.

Note

A more substantial dish, very good indeed, is made with slices of cooked pork sausage, placed on the toasted mustard bread, over which you pour the cheese and apple, melted in cider.

West Country Fondue

serves 4–6 as a starter or cheese course

200g (7oz) Somerset Brie
200g (7oz) Ticklemore Goat cheese
200g (7oz) Devon Garland cheese
350ml (12fl oz) dry West Country cider
1 apple, peeled, cored and grated (optional)
grating of nutmeg
2–3 tablespoons Somerset cider brandy

Remove the rind from the cheeses and spoon or grate it into a non-stick saucepan. Add the cider and apple, if using it. Cook gently until the cheese melts into the cider. Bring to the boil, season with nutmeg, and pour in the brandy.

Bring to the table bubbling, and eat it from the pot.

Toasted cubes or batons of saffron bread make it a very nice accompaniment when served at the end of the meal; otherwise, use plain bread.

Hot Potted Cheese | serves 6–8

4 tablespoons fresh white breadcrumbs
4 tablespoons port or sweet oloroso sherry
225g (8oz) grated hard cheese
85g (3oz) butter, softened
4 free-range eggs, separated
freshly ground black pepper

Soak the breadcrumbs in the port or sherry for a few minutes. Drain them and mix with the cheese and softened butter. Mix in the egg yolks, season and then fold in the stiffly whisked egg whites. Spoon into buttered ramekins and bake in a preheated oven at 180°C/350°F/Gas 4 for about 15–20 minutes.

Some West Country Flavours Preserved

If you have the time, using fruit you've gathered in the hedgerows, windfall apples or sharp crabs, scented garden flowers and those you gather in the wild, to make small pots of jellies and preserves is very rewarding. They make lovely gifts.

Here are a few of my favourite recipes, starting with elderflowers, which are usually the first to urge me to bring out the preserving pan. When we drove down to Cornwall one hot June day, I couldn't wait until we reached the Mill, but had Tom stop the car halfway down the stony track so that I could gather armfuls of the delicate creamy panicles. Trethew Elderflower Cordial is dispensed with considerable parsimony; it makes a wonderfully refreshing drink mixed with sparkling mineral water, a fine cocktail or aperitif mixed with gin and sparkling water, and is excellent to flavour custards and ice creams.

Elderflower Sparkler | makes about 4 litres (8 pints)

6 large elderflower heads
450g (1lb) granulated sugar
1 lemon
2 tablespoons white wine vinegar
4 litres (8 pints) still cold water, bottled or from the tap, as you prefer

Use a large bowl, and place the flower heads in it. Add the sugar, the thinly pared zest of the lemon, its juice and half the lemon skin, the vinegar and water. Cover loosely, and leave for 24–36 hours.

Strain through fine cheesecloth, or muslin, and bottle in screw-top or corked bottles. Leave for 3 weeks before serving chilled.

Alternatively, make elderflower syrup or cordial, and dilute it with sparkling mineral water.

Elderflower Cordial | makes about 1.25 litres (2 pints)

about 1kg (generous 2lb) granulated sugar
1.25 litres (2 pints) water
15 elderflower heads, well shaken, stalks removed
2 oranges, thinly sliced
2 lemons, thinly sliced
2 limes, thinly sliced
25g (1oz) tartaric acid

Put the sugar and water into a saucepan, dissolve the sugar over a gentle heat, then bring it to the boil. Drop in the flower heads, and bring back to the boil. Put the fruit slices into a bowl or large jug with the tartaric acid, and pour on the syrup and flowers. Stir well, cover loosely, and leave for 24 hours before bottling. Keeps for 2–3 months or longer if refrigerated.

Elderflower custard is delicious with the Gooseberry and Almond Crumble recipe on page 256.

Elderflower Milk Punch | serves 4–6

4 elderflower heads
1–2 tablespoons clear honey or sugar
½ lemon, seeded and thinly sliced
3–4 tablespoons cognac
600ml (1 pint) milk
freshly grated nutmeg

Strip the elderflowers from the stems. Rinse thoroughly, drain, and put into a bowl with the honey or sugar, lemon slices and cognac. Scald the milk, and pour it over the ingredients in the bowl. Flavour with nutmeg and leave to stand until cool. Strain into glasses, and serve.

Note

It is also very good as a hot punch, but the flavours have longer to develop if the milk is allowed to cool.

Lavender Cordial | makes about 500ml (18fl oz)

20 lavender heads
500ml (18fl oz) bottle of brandy or cognac
115–175g (4–6oz) sugar, or to taste, dissolved to a syrup in 2–3 tablespoons water

Shake the lavender, strip off the flowers, and put them into a preserving jar. Pour in the brandy or cognac, seal, and leave for 2–3 months in a dark place.

Strain the brandy or cognac into a bowl, and stir in the sugar syrup. Bottle and label.

Well-set Strawberry Preserve

For each 500g (generous 1lb) strawberries, hulled, rinsed and placed in a bowl, cover with 500g (generous 1lb) sugar and 2 tablespoons hot water. Leave overnight.

The next day, strain the syrup into a saucepan with 85ml (3fl oz) water, and boil for 5–10 minutes. Add to the strawberries 1 tablespoon frozen cranberries, stapled into a damp coffee filter to make a packet, and boil until the fruit and syrup jell. Remove the packet of cranberries. If you prefer, you can cook them into the jam, in which case they should be cooked first with a small amount of water, crushed and then added to the syrup with the strawberries, otherwise the skins will remain tough. Spoon the jam into clean, hot, dry jars. Seal and label.

Rose Petal Jelly | makes about 1kg (2lb)

While you have the jam pan and all the accoutrements of jam-making to hand, and if you are lucky enough to be able to get heavily scented roses, try this delightfully old-fashioned teatime speciality. It makes wonderful presents.

1kg (generous 2lb) cooking apples
sugar
600 ml (1 pint) or more dark red scented rose petals

Wash and chop the uncored apples, and put into a saucepan. Add enough water to cover them by 2.5cm (1in) or so. Cook until the fruit is soft. Mash the fruit to extract as much juice and pectin as possible. Strain through a jelly bag for several hours or overnight.

Measure the volume of the liquid, and then measure out an equal quantity of sugar. Pound half the rose petals in a small quantity of the sugar, and mix with the juice and the rest of the sugar. Put into a preserving pan or heavy saucepan. Keep the rest of the petals to add later. Heat the pan gently, and stir until the sugar has dissolved. Add the remaining rose petals, and bring the syrup to boiling point. Boil fast until setting point is reached, and pot in small, clean, hot jam jars. Seal and label.

Hedgerow Jelly

While you still have the preserving pan out, you might think about making a few small jars of hedgerow jelly. Crab apples, windfalls and damsons (with a few cracked kernels) can all be added to produce a lovely rich purple jelly. Mix the fruit or keep in single batches if you have rich pickings.

Use whatever edible wild berries, fruits, hips and haws you can find, and if possible, use those of the same colour to give red or purple jellies. On the other hand, real foragers will not be too bothered about this nicety and will use a handful of this and a portion of that. Most of these wild fruits are sour and indeed quite inedible unless cooked with sugar, and they have enough pectin to give them a set. Elderberries need added pectin, which is best obtained from windfall apples, cookers or crabs, or freeze them until you can get the first of the cranberries. Hips, haws and rowan berries are not very juicy, and again, it is a good plan to cook them with apples to give extra juice.

The ingredients could not be simpler: you need the fruit, a little water and, at the next stage, sugar. Cook the fruit until soft. The juiciest fruit needs only 2.5cm (1in) or so of water in the pan, drier fruit should have about half its volume of water, and the hardest fruit should be almost covered with water. When the fruit is soft, mash it to extract all the pulp and essences. Suspend a jelly bag, and let the pulp drip through it overnight. Measure out the juice, and for each 600ml (1 pint), measure out an equal volume of sugar. Put both into a saucepan, and heat gently until the sugar has dissolved. Then boil fast until setting point is reached. Pot in small, clean, hot, dry jars; seal and label.

If you have only a small amount of fruit and want to make spiced jelly to serve with game, cook the fruit with cider vinegar rather than with water and a cinnamon stick, a couple of cloves and a few cardamom pods. This is an excellent way of using windfall apples.

Damson Cheese

This is an excellent preserve made from damsons that will repay keeping until Christmas. By then, it will be beginning to shrink away from the sides of its container, and the sugar may start to crystallize on the surface and at the edges. These are signs not of deterioration but that all is well. The batch of damson cheese I made one September did not last beyond a few autumn dinners and lunches, when I served it with farmhouse cheeses.

If you have a damson tree, you will probably be inclined to make much more damson cheese than if you have to buy the fruit, and I have not given overall quantities. Use 450g (1lb) sugar for each 450g (1lb) fruit purée.

damsons
water
sugar

Wash the damsons and put them into a saucepan with about 2.5cm (1in) or so of water in the bottom to stop the fruit from sticking before the juices have been released. Cook the fruit until soft. Rub through a sieve, weigh the pulp, and make a note of it. Weigh out an equal quantity of sugar. Crack some of the kernels, and add these to the pulp for flavour.

Put the purée into a saucepan, and cook to reduce it by a quarter to a third in order to remove some of the water content. Meanwhile, warm the sugar, then add it to the fruit purée.

Stir over a low heat until the sugar has dissolved, then cook until the mixture thickens sufficiently to part when a spoon is drawn through it. Pack into straight-sided pots, loaf tins or flat, round Victoria sponge tins, and leave overnight to set. The pots can then be covered and sealed. The cheese set in a loaf tin or sponge tin can be turned out and closely wrapped in waxed paper and kitchen foil for storage.

Note

Quince and apple cheese can be made in the same way. Time-consuming to make, but well worth it for lovely Christmas presents, they are economical in that they use the pulp left over after making quince and apple jelly. Quince or apple alone can be used, depending on availability, but just as the two fruits combine well in pies, so they do in these jellies. Sieving the pulp is the hardest part of the recipe.

Spiced Pickled Pears

600ml (1 pint) red wine vinegar
675g (1½lb) sugar
5cm (2in) cinnamon stick
12 allspice berries
12 cloves
½ teaspoon blade mace
2 bay leaves
about 1kg (2lb) Conference pears or another firm variety

Put all the ingredients, except the pears, into a saucepan. Heat gently until the sugar has melted, then bring to the boil.

Meanwhile, quarter, peel and core the pears, and place them in a large bowl. Pour the liquid over them, cover and leave overnight. Strain the liquid back into a saucepan, and boil it for 10–12 minutes to reduce the volume since the pears will have given off some liquid. Pour it over the fruit, and allow to stand for half a day.

Boil the fruit and syrup together for 30 seconds. With a slotted spoon, remove the pears, and pack into clean, hot, dry preserving jars. Reboil the syrup, pour it over the pears, and seal the jars immediately. Allow to cool, label and store. Keep for at least 3 weeks before using.

Somerset Fig and Apple Mincemeat

makes about 2kg (4lb)

When carol singers come calling for their traditional 'figgy pudding', give them mince pies, made from this deliciously rich-tasting mincemeat. It will keep very well, since fresh apple – 1 peeled, cored and grated Bramley for about 1kg (2lb) mincemeat – is only added when you want to make the mincepies.

500g (generous 1lb) dried figs
500g (generous 1lb) dried apples (not apple crisps, but the leather rings of dried fruit)
500g (generous 1lb) mixed vine fruit
200g (7oz) candied peel, chopped
150g (5oz) walnuts or almonds, chopped
150g (5oz) light muscovado sugar
150ml (¼ pint) Somerset cider brandy
150g (5oz) vegetarian suet, or coarsely grated, chilled, creamed coconut
1 teaspoon each ground cinnamon and aniseed

Remove the stalk end of the figs, and roughly chop them and the apples. Put them and the vine fruit into a food processor, and process to the texture you prefer.

Transfer the mixture to a bowl, and mix in the rest of the ingredients by hand. Leave overnight for the flavours to blend, then spoon into clean jars, cover, seal and label.

Gooseberry Chutney | makes about 2kg (4lb)

about 2kg (4lb) gooseberries, topped and tailed
1 large Bramley apple, peeled, cored and sliced
1 large mild onion, peeled and chopped
600ml (1 pint) spiced malt vinegar
900g (2lb) light muscovado or demerara sugar
1 teaspoon each freshly ground black pepper, cinnamon, cardamom and cloves
450g (1lb) raisins

Cook the gooseberries, apple and onion to a pulp in the vinegar. Stir in the sugar, and when it has dissolved, add rest of the ingredients, and cook until thick. Pot while hot in clean, hot, dry jars. Seal and label.

Gooseberry Vinegar

450g (1lb) gooseberries, 6–12 of them topped, tailed and poached, for garnish
2 shallots, peeled and chopped
2 garlic cloves, peeled and crushed
1 tablespoon light muscovado or demerara sugar
300ml (½ pint) white wine or vinegar or cider vinegar

Reserve the topped and tailed gooseberries. Crush the rest, and mix in the remaining ingredients. Leave overnight, if you can, or for at least an hour or two. Strain and bottle.

A Selection of Flower Vinegars | makes 4 bottles

4 bottles of white wine vinegar
8 sprigs of lavender
2 elderflower heads
2 fragrant red or pink roses
8–10 clove pinks

Soak off the labels without opening the bottles. Shake the flowers to remove any insects or loose pollen. Trim the lavender to about 12.5cm (5in) of stalk. Break up the elderflower heads into small sprigs. Remove the petals from the roses and pinks, keeping them separate. Put the flowers into the vinegar bottles, screw on the tops, or cork the bottles. Label simply, and stand them on a sunny windowsill.

After a week or so, strain each vinegar, and replace the flowers with fresh ones. Recork, and stick on permanent labels. If you still have the vinegar the following year (the lavender vinegar seems to keep particularly well), remove the old flowers and add fresh ones. Herb-flavoured vinegars are made in exactly the same way. I generally use white wine vinegar because I like to see the contents of the bottle. But elderflowers are very good in cider vinegar, and there is no reason not to use red wine vinegar if you wish to make a fragrant red rose vinegar.

Cider

Sweet Hoary Morning, Slack-ma-girdle, Whimple Honeydrop and Fair Maid of Devon are not West Country folk songs but some of the more than fifty varieties of cider apple known to have been grown in Cornwall and on the Devon border, documented by the Avon Cider Apple Consultancy. Kent and Sussex were really the cradle of cider production in England where it was introduced by the Normans. Cider production was further developed by the first Viscount Scudamore when he retired from Charles I's court to his estates in Herefordshire where he devoted his time to perfecting the cultivation of cider apples. Since then the growing of cider apples spread to the Midlands and the south-west of England.

The apples used are not like our dessert and cooking apples. They are smaller, usually, and although some are sweet, many are bittersweet, bittersharp or sharp, and good cider will be made from a careful blend of the fermented juices of the apples after they are harvested in September.

In Somerset, too, the distillation of cider is being carried out, to produce an excellent apple or cider spirit, called cider brandy. The brandy-makers of Jerez in Spain are not too happy about that, however; they feel that only grape-based spirits should be called brandy.

The cider-making process, both past and present, can be seen at some of the West Country's cider farms, such as the Callestock Cider Farm near Truro (see Gazetteer for details).

I find cider brandy, like saffron, clotted cream and honey, essential in my West Country kitchen. Cider is immensely versatile and can be used in sweet and savoury dishes, with meat as well as with fish and shellfish, and with fruit. Many favourite recipes which call for wine can just as well take cider, whether sweet or dry, still or sparkling. And it is, of course, an excellent accompaniment to the cheeses of the West Country, served with some homemade bread and chutney.

A Country Christmas

Christmas is the one time of the year when even those who do not normally like to cook are willing to spend time in the kitchen to produce seasonal treats for family and friends. But I promise you, it needn't be an effort. On the contrary, it can be easy, stress-free and enjoyable.

I have developed a collection of Christmas recipes that include some extremely easy and quick puddings and starters, and centrepiece main courses that look after themselves once in the oven. I also include some suggestions on what to do with leftovers. Some of the recipes are entirely traditional, some use traditional ingredients in not quite traditional ways, and some are not at all traditional but I feel they fit in well with Christmas cookery.

Celery, Blue Cheese and Chestnut Soup

serves 6–8

1 onion, peeled and sliced
1 medium head of celery, trimmed, washed and sliced
12 chestnuts, peeled
55g (2oz) butter
600ml (1 pint) semi-skimmed milk
1.2 litres (2 pints) chicken or vegetable stock
175g (6oz) West Country blue cheese, crumbled
freshly grated nutmeg
white pepper

Cook the onion, celery and chestnuts in the butter for 5–10 minutes, then add the milk, and simmer until the chestnuts are tender. Add half the stock and the crumbled cheese. Allow to cool slightly before blending and sieving the mixture into the saucepan.

Add the rest of the stock, bring to the boil, and season. Cream can be swirled in before serving, if you wish, and the soup garnished with a sprinkling of chopped dried cranberries.

A Crisp Winter Salad

With so much rich food on the table at Christmas, I like to keep my starters small, or at least crisp and fresh. And nothing could be fresher than a winter salad. At this time of year we are lucky enough to be able to get the various chicories with their bitter leaves. Look for witloof, the pale yellow and white plump oval chicory, radicchio with its strong crimson colour, and whatever other varieties you can find. I like to partner these with sweet, anise-flavoured fennel, crisp, nutty celery and the sweet and slightly peppery kohl rabi. I cut the vegetables variously into wedges and slices as appropriate, and tear off the leaves. I prefer to hand round the dressing separately, in case there are others like me who prefer to eat the salad au naturel.

Herb, Walnut and Lemon Dressing for Winter Salad

1 tablespoon finely chopped fresh chives
1 tablespoon finely chopped fresh parsley
1 teaspoon fresh thyme leaves
2 garlic cloves, peeled and chopped
55g (2oz) walnuts, chopped
½ teaspoon sea salt
freshly ground black pepper
50ml (2floz) walnut oil
150ml (¼ pint) sunflower or grapeseed oil
juice of ½ lemon

Mix the herbs together in a bowl. Crush the garlic and walnuts with the salt, and mix into the herbs. Add pepper to taste, then slowly add the oils and finally the lemon juice. This will keep, refrigerated, for a few days.

Roasted Aubergine, Pepper, Olive and Parsnip Terrine | serves 6–8

If you want a more substantial starter than a salad, but still vegetable-based, try this colourful terrine of sliced vegetables which are roasted or grilled to a sweet tenderness before being packed into a terrine. We had extra vegetables left over which were very good with a little salad dressing, and the crisp roasted parsnip slices were a marvellous and unexpected companion to some Parma ham.

2 large aubergines
2–3 parsnips, peeled
4 red peppers
2 yellow peppers
extra virgin olive oil
small jar of black olive paste
1 leaf of gelatine, softened in cold water and then dissolved in 150ml (¼ pint) well-seasoned vegetable stock

Slice the aubergines and parsnips lengthways. Quarter the peppers, and remove the seeds and pith. Brush the vegetables lightly with oil, and roast in a preheated oven at 200°C/400°F/Gas6 until tender, or cook on a griddle, or under a grill. The peppers should be charred, and then, when cool enough to handle, skinned. Layer the vegetables in a loaf tin, starting with a layer of aubergines, then red peppers, parsnips, yellow peppers, parsnips, red peppers, and finally aubergine on top, spreading a little olive paste on each layer.

Pour on the gelatine stock, and let the vegetables absorb it for 20–30 minutes. Then cover the terrine with clingfilm, and drain off most of the excess liquid. Refrigerate overnight, turn out, and slice.

Warm Leek and Smoked Salmon Salad

serves 4–6

Here is a recipe I wrote down in my brother's kitchen when I was last in Hong Kong. He cooked an impromptu dinner for us from ingredients he had bought on his way home from work, and I think it makes an absolutely splendid quick starter for Christmas.

350g (12oz) slim, young leeks
115g (4oz) button, cap or oyster mushrooms
extra virgin olive oil
small salad leaves
225g (8oz) smoked salmon
lemon juice, to taste
freshly ground black pepper

For the garnish
black olives

Peel and trim the leeks, and slice them. Rinse thoroughly, and drain them. Wipe and slice the mushrooms, or if oyster mushrooms, tear them into wedges. Heat the oil in a frying pan (2–3 tablespoons will be sufficient), and gently cook the leeks until wilted and almost tender. Then add the mushrooms, and continue cooking until just done. Meanwhile, arrange salad leaves on serving plates. Cut the smoked salmon into strips, and quickly toss it with the leeks and mushrooms in the pan before spooning it on to the plate. Season with lemon juice and pepper, and pour the cooking juices over the salad before serving. Add the olives.

Note

A variation of this replaces the leeks and mushrooms with slim green beans and waxy salad potatoes, which are steamed or boiled instead of fried.

Warm Christmas Salad | serves 6–8

1 turkey, duck or goose liver
225g (8oz) chicken livers
2 tablespoons groundnut or sunflower oil
225g (8oz) oyster or white button mushrooms
85g (3oz) cranberries
1 round fennel bulb
juice of 1 lemon
salad leaves
fresh herbs
225g (8oz) peeled prawns
1 pomegranate
2–3 tablespoons raspberry or balsamic vinegar
75ml (⅛ pint) extra virgin olive oil

Trim the livers, removing any green bilestained parts and threads of gristle. Fry them in the oil until just cooked but still pink inside. Transfer to a plate. Slice the mushrooms, and fry very briefly in the same pan until just wilted. Poach the cranberries for 2–3 minutes in a little water, then drain. Trim the fennel, and slice into rings or slivers, and sprinkle with lemon juice.

Arrange salad leaves and fresh herbs on a large platter or individual plates. Arrange the fennel around the outer edge, and then the mushrooms. Place the prawns on top. Slice the livers, and arrange these before garnishing with cranberries and pomegranate seeds. Deglaze the frying pan with the vinegar, and combine it with the oil. Mix and spoon over the salad.

Note

You can also use the gizzard and heart of the bird, cooked in the same way as the liver, although the gizzard is best sliced first and then cooked.

Potted Smoked Salmon | serves 6–8 as a starter

225g (8oz) smoked salmon (offcuts will do)
175g (6oz) unsalted butter, softened
juice of 1 lemon
good pinch of ground mace
fine sea salt
freshly ground black pepper

Put the pieces of smoked salmon and butter into a food processor, and blend until smooth. Season to taste with lemon juice, mace, salt and pepper.

Spoon the mixture into ramekins, garnish with herbs if you like, and chill until ready to serve. If you want to keep this for a week or so, cover with a layer of clarified butter, which will seal it.

Variations

Lobster, crayfish, sardines, shrimps, oysters, smoked trout and mackerel.

For potted sardines, mix in a little grated apple, a few finely chopped shallots, and a sparkling of finely chopped fresh dill.

For devilled potted shrimps, season with salt, cayenne pepper and lemon juice.

For potted oysters, use shucked and drained raw oysters, thoroughly dried on a tea-towel, and pound them into the butter, together with 2 anchovy fillets to every 6 oysters. Season with mace or nutmeg and lemon juice. Potted oysters should be treated in the same way as raw oysters. They should be eaten within a few hours of preparation, and they should *not* be kept overnight, even in a refrigerator.

Potted smoked fish is very good served with a cucumber and horseradish relish. Make this by mixing the finely chopped flesh of a medium-sized cucumber with 4 finely chopped spring onions, 3 finely chopped sprigs of mint, and a tablespoon of grated horseradish. Stir this into 150ml (¼ pint) thick Greek yoghurt, and season to taste with freshly ground black pepper.

Herb Griddle Cakes with Horseradish and Salmon Roe | makes about 18

175g (6oz) plain flour
1 generous teaspoon baking powder
300ml (½ pint) milk
1 tablespoon plain yoghurt
1 free-range egg
1 heaped tablespoon finely chopped fresh herbs, including chives
150g (5oz) mascarpone
fresh horseradish, to taste
jar of salmon roe

Mix the first 6 ingredients to a smooth batter, and drop soup-spoonfuls on to a well-seasoned griddle or frying pan. Cook on both sides. Mix the mascarpone and horseradish and spread on the warm griddle cakes. Top with salmon roe.

Note

As an alternative, use slivers of smoked salmon or flaked smoked trout.

Prawns in Saffron Cream | serves 6–8

Serve this dish as a starter in a 'cup' of lettuce, or as an appetizer in chicory leaves. It is also very good served with a halved sliced avocado. Fresh orange juice and zest are very good with shellfish, and make a change from lemon. It is even better if you can get Seville oranges, but they do not usually reach us until after Christmas.

1kg (generous 2lb) prawns in the shell
good pinch of saffron strands
450ml (¾ pint) double cream
150ml (¼ pint) plain yoghurt, crème fraiche or soured cream
fresh chervil, chives or parsley
sea salt and freshly ground black pepper
1–2 teaspoons grated orange or tangerine zest

Peel the prawns and put the shells into a saucepan with about 300ml (½ pint) water. Boil for 5–10 minutes, strain and reduce by half. Infuse the saffron in 2 tablespoons of the shellfish stock. Whip the cream until stiff, fold in the yoghurt and the saffron liquid and whisk once more.

Stir in the herbs and prawns and season to taste with salt, pepper and orange or tangerine zest.

Baked Oysters and Horseradish in Potatoes

makes 12

This dish is quite substantial, and I would particularly recommend it if you plan a cold main course, perhaps a cold buffet on Boxing Day. The recipe is also most versatile. If you choose not to use oysters, you can substitute prawns, mushrooms or mussels. Often I bake quail eggs in the hollowed-out potatoes.

12 small potatoes, weighing about 55g (2oz) each
55g (2oz) unsalted butter, melted
sea salt and freshly ground black pepper
55g (2oz) creamed or grated horseradish
12 raw oysters

Wash and scrub the potatoes. If new, they should not need peeling. With a melon baller, scoop out in each potato a hollow large enough to hold an oyster, and remove a very thin slice from the bottom to allow it to stand flat. Put the hollowed-out potatoes into a pan of salted water, bring to the boil, and boil briskly until just cooked. Drain.

Brush the potatoes inside and out with melted butter, season lightly with salt and pepper, put a little horseradish into each and stand them on an oiled baking tray. Put an oyster into each potato. Place in the top half of a preheated oven at 180°C/350°F/Gas4, and bake for 8–10 minutes. Serve immediately, with lemon wedges and a pepper grinder.

Turkey Popovers | makes 12–18

Good as snacks, elevenses, or canapés with drinks, 2–3 popovers, served on a plate with a small dressed salad, make a good starter and are an excellent way of using leftover turkey, as in the following recipe.

2 free-range eggs
115g (4oz) plain flour
300ml (½ pint) milk
55g (2oz) butter
225g (8oz) diced, cooked turkey meat
115g (4oz) diced, cooked stuffing
cranberry sauce made from whole cranberries (optional)

Make a smooth batter with the eggs, flour and milk. Grease deep bun tins with turkey dripping, if you have any, otherwise with butter, and put a little of the batter into each hollow. Put in a preheated oven at 200°C/400°F/Gas6, for 5 minutes. Stir the turkey and stuffing into the remaining batter. When the tin is very hot, spoon in the batter to about two-thirds full, and return to the oven.

Bake for about 15–20 minutes until puffed up and deep golden-brown. Remove from the oven and serve with a little cranberry sauce in the middle of each popover.

Cranberry-glazed Turkey Tartlets | makes 12–18

225g (8oz) shortcrust pastry
115g (4oz) turkey stuffing
225g (8oz) cooked turkey, diced or shredded
85g (3oz) toasted pine kernels, or chopped walnuts
55g (2oz) dried cranberries or sultanas, chopped
pinch of ground cinnamon
pinch of ground cloves
1 teaspoon sugar
6 tablespoons turkey gravy or stock
1 free-range egg yolk
3–4 tablespoons double cream
3 tablespoons cranberry jelly, for glazing

Line tartlet tins with the pastry, prick the bases and bake blind in a preheated oven at 180°C/350°F/Gas 4 for 10 minutes. Remove from the oven, and allow to cool slightly. Crumble the stuffing and place in the bottom of each tartlet case. Mix the turkey with the rest of the ingredients, and spoon into the tarts. Smooth the surface. Put the cranberry jelly into a saucepan with a tablespoon of water, and heat until the jelly has melted. Brush liberally over the turkey, and bake for a further 10–15 minutes at the same oven temperature.

Remove from the oven and allow to cool, then re-glaze with the remaining jelly, allowing it to set before serving.

Little Game Pies | makes 24 individual pies

These small pies make lovely appetizers or savouries to hand round with drinks, and, in their sweet/savoury combination, are not unlike the original mince pie.

450g (1lb) cooked meat off the bone, rabbit, grouse, pigeon or venison or a mixture
85g (3oz) raisins
85g (3oz) sultanas
1 apple, peeled, cored and chopped
85g (3oz) pine kernels or blanched almonds, chopped
85g (3oz) light muscovado sugar
grated zest and juice of 1 lemon
300ml (½ pint) game stock, gravy or cooking juices
1 small onion, peeled and finely chopped
1 tablespoon finely chopped fresh parsley
sea salt and freshly ground black pepper
ground mace or freshly grated nutmeg
ground allspice
350g (12oz) plain shortcrust pastry
beaten free-range egg and milk, to glaze

Chop the meat and put into a bowl with the dried fruit, apple, nuts, sugar, lemon, stock, onion and parsley. Add salt, pepper and spices to taste, bearing in mind that dishes served cold often need a little more seasoning than those served hot.

Roll out the pastry, and use two-thirds to line 24 bun tins. Spoon in the filling, and cover with pastry lids cut from the remaining pastry. Brush with the egg and milk, and bake in a preheated oven at 180°C/350°F/Gas 4 for 35–40 minutes.

Main Courses

In the second programme in my West Country Christmas series I concentrated on the main course. A traditional roast turkey with an unfamiliar twist and a succulent joint of pork with tropical fruit provided leftovers which, when added to other seasonal ingredients such as chestnuts and cranberries, can be turned into a magnificent medieval-style Christmas pie, perfect for Boxing Day.

Herb-seasoned Roast Turkey | serves 6–8

In France, it is traditional to cook the Christmas turkey with thin slices of truffle under the skin. Here is a less expensive, yet equally good version. I like to use tarragon, basil, flat-leaf parsley, chervil and coriander, rather than the very pungent herbs such as sage and rosemary.

3.5kg (about 8lb) very fresh free-range organic turkey
100g (3½oz) softened butter
115g (4oz) fresh herbs on the stem
4–5 garlic cloves, peeled and thinly sliced (optional)
1 tablespoon each sea salt and freshly ground black pepper
1 lemon

Remove any visible fat from the turkey cavity. Ease the skin away from the flesh by gradually inserting your fingers between the skin and the breasts. Continue working your way round the bird until the skin is loose around the legs and back. Spread butter over the flesh, then stuff the space with the herbs, arranging the leaves over the surface of the turkey and under the skin. Do the same with the garlic slices, if you are using them. This is all much easier than it sounds.

Rub the salt and pepper over the turkey and season inside. Prick the lemon all over with a skewer and put it into the cavity with any remaining herbs. Cover the bird loosely, but carefully, with kitchen foil or clingfilm, and refrigerate for 24 hours.

When you are ready to cook it, bring the turkey back to room temperature, and roast in a preheated oven at 200°C/400°F/Gas 6 for about 3 hours.

Note

If you make stock from the leftovers and turkey carcase, you can really only use it for soup. Do not try to reduce it to make sauce as it would be far too salty. A very tasty soup can be produced by cooking rice in the stock, adding a little grated lemon zest, a hint of lemon juice, some leftover cooked turkey, and, right at the end, without letting it boil, an egg yolk, well beaten, with a little single cream. You will then have something like the Greek *avgolemono* soup.

Steamed Turkey Breast Stuffed with Oysters and Wild Mushrooms | serves 4–6

The unusual combination of 2 traditional Christmas ingredients, turkey and oysters, makes an excellent alternative to the whole roast bird with all the trimmings. It is especially suitable for a Christmas lunch for 2–4 people when a large golden turkey with all the trimmings would overwhelm. Nevertheless, it is worth buying a whole bird because the rest of it – legs, thighs and wings – can be boned, diced, and made into a spicy Moroccan-style stew or *tagine* for a supper over the Christmas holidays. Add prunes or dried apricots, almonds or pine kernels and chopped lemon for an authentic touch. Serve with steamed couscous or bulgur wheat scattered with fresh coriander. Use the carcase to make stock.

The breasts from a 3.5kg (8 lb) turkey will feed 4–6 people in this recipe. If you cannot get fresh oysters or do not like them, use extra mushrooms in the stuffing. These can be shitake or oyster mushrooms, ceps or chanterelles, if you can find them, or dried wild mushrooms.

The basic recipe is open to many interpretations. Chicken or capon can be prepared in this way. Instead of a mushroom and oyster stuffing, use lightly cooked, pencil-thin leeks, strips of courgette and carrot batons for a colourful, light stuffing, very attractive when the meat is sliced. However, I think the combination of turkey and oysters is very hard to beat.

55g (2oz) fennel bulb, peeled and diced
55g (2oz) celery or celeriac, peeled and diced
2 turkey breasts
2 tablespoons double cream
1 tablespoon thick plain yoghurt or fromage frais
sea salt and freshly ground black pepper
turkey liver, lightly fried
6 oysters
25g (1oz) dried wild mushrooms soaked and precooked with the cooking liquor reserved, or 115g (4oz) fresh mushrooms, lightly fried or blanched
150ml (¼ pint) stock
4 tablespoons good dry white wine

Put the fennel and celery or celeriac into a small saucepan. Cover with water or stock, and simmer until soft. Drain and reserve any cooking liquid. Remove the skin from the turkey breasts, and take off the long, narrow fillet of meat which is easily detached. With a sharp knife, remove the white sinew from the fillets, and cut them into pieces. Put into a food processor with the soft vegetables, cream, yoghurt or fromage frais, salt and pepper. Process until you have an entirely smooth soft paste.

Carefully open out the turkey breasts by slipping in a sharp knife horizontally, and working through the flesh without quite separating it into 2 slices. You should be able to open out the meat, butterfly style. Flatten slightly by covering with clingfilm, and rolling with a rolling pin. Do not beat the meat, or you will risk tearing it. Spread the mousse over the meat. Cut the turkey liver into several long strips, and lay these along the length of each breast, on one half only.

Carefully remove the oysters from their shells, straining the liquor into the cooking juices reserved earlier. Lay 3 oysters down the centre of each opened-out turkey breast. Keep half the mushrooms for the sauce, and arrange the rest on the turkey breasts. Open out 2 roasting bags to wrap the meat for steaming.

Transfer each turkey breast carefully to the wrap, and fold over the meat, then gradually roll it by folding one half of the wrap over the meat, and rolling the whole thing over. Twist the ends of the parcel, and tuck underneath. You should have 2 neat rolls of filled meat.

Place in a steamer basket, lower over boiling water, cover with a lid, and steam for about 15 minutes. Remove, and allow to rest in a warm place for 10–15 minutes or so, which makes the turkey easier to slice.

Meanwhile, make the sauce by boiling together the juices from the vegetables, the oysters and the mushrooms with the stock and wine and reducing until you have a well-flavoured, shiny, but not sticky, sauce. Add the mushrooms. (It would be a pity to enrich it with butter since this is such a light, healthy dish, using low-fat meat and cooked by steaming.) Slice the meat, and serve with the sauce spooned around it.

This is very good with wild rice and some crisp, green vegetables, such a stir-fried cabbage or broccoli.

Turkey Fillets with Pomegranate Sauce

serves 4

You should start the preparation for this dish the day before, with the marinade. The meat can be grilled, chargrilled or cooked in a heavy cast-iron pan. I prefer the latter because any cooking juices are gathered up for when you make the sauce.

4 × 175g (6oz) turkey fillets, sliced from the breast
3–4 ripe pomegranates
1 tablespoon walnut oil
2 garlic cloves, peeled and crushed
½ teaspoon juniper berries
¼ teaspoon ground cardamom
¼ teaspoon ground cumin
25g (1oz) butter
300ml (½ pint) turkey stock made from the carcase
salt and freshly ground black pepper

For the garnish
fresh walnut halves

Slightly flatten the turkey fillets, and place in a single layer in a shallow dish. Cut the pomegranates in half. Remove about 30–40 whole seeds, and reserve these for garnish. Squeeze the pomegranate halves, as you would lemons, to extract as much juice as possible. Sieve into a bowl or jug. Stir in the walnut oil, garlic, juniper berries, cardamom and cumin. Pour over the meat, cover, and marinate overnight.

When you are ready to cook the turkey fillets, remove them from the marinade, which you put to one side. Dry the meat on kitchen paper. Melt half the butter in a large, heavy frying pan, and when nut-brown, place the turkey fillets in a single layer in the pan. Cook over a fairly high heat to brown the meat nicely, then turn down the heat and cook for about 4–5 minutes. Raise the heat again, turn the meat over, and brown on the other side. Lower the heat, and cook gently until the meat is done, 4–5 minutes, depending on the thickness of the meat.

Remove the fillets from the pan, and keep them warm on a covered plate while you finish the sauce. Raise the heat, pour in the marinade and the stock, and let it bubble away until reduced by half. Make sure you scrape up all the bits stuck to the bottom of the pan. Cut the rest of the butter into pieces, and add them one at a time to the sauce. Season to taste. Divide the sauce among 4 heated dinner plates, arrange the turkey fillet on top, sliced or not, as you please. Garnish with 2–3 walnut halves and the pomegranate seeds.

Serve this beautifully festive-looking dish with, perhaps, a crisp fennel salad, some broccoli and a purée of potatoes and garlic with cardamom seeds.

Goose for Two

For years I hesitated to buy a goose for Christmas for just the two of us, as it always seemed so extravagantly large. But for the last two or three years, I have ordered and cooked one, and we have enjoyed it greatly, although there is still enough left over for a number of dishes. I now have the solution, which I devised a few years ago. When we finished filming the Christmas series, I was not at all sure that I wanted to cook another turkey, so I put in an order for a goose from Swaddles Green Farm. I'm not sure that Charlotte Reynolds approved of what I planned to do with the bird, but I really find it an ideal method for two. I also like what I can do with the rest of the goose.

For the Christmas roast, I dismantle the goose, leaving the breast intact and on the bone. Do this by first removing the legs, cutting through the ball and socket joint. Next remove the wings, as close to the body as you can. With a pair of good sharp poultry shears, separate the breast from the back, cutting from the vent end to the neck on both sides of the breast. The two unequal halves are now separated, the back for stock and the breast to roast. This is a very handsome piece of meat when roasted, like a golden-brown cushion.

1 goose breast, about 1.35–1.8kg (3–4lb)
2 tablespoons clear honey

2 tablespoons fino or amontillado sherry
1 tablespoon sherry or cider vinegar
1 teaspoon freshly ground black pepper

Line the roasting tin with kitchen foil to come up the sides. Prick the skin of the goose breast all over, down through the thickness of fat, but without piercing the flesh too much. Melt the honey in a saucepan, and mix in the rest of the ingredients. Brush over the breast, and roast on the middle shelf of a preheated oven at 180°C/350°F/Gas4, for about 20 minutes per 450g (1lb). Periodically, drain off the fat, and baste the bird with the honey mixture. This gives it a nice glaze and a subtle flavour. There is, of course, a whole range of basting/flavouring combinations you might like to try – cider and honey, soy sauce and mirin (rice wine), mandarin or lemon juice and herbs – or indeed, you may prefer to leave it unflavoured. A handful of herbs, such as sage under the ribcage, as it roasts, will flavour the goose delicately.

As with any traditional roast, potatoes can be cooked around the meat and will absorb some of the lovely goose fat. Baked onions also go well with goose. As for other accompanying vegetables, I am much more partial to a green salad afterwards, or a vegetable course to begin with, such as celery and chestnut soup.

Note

Goose fat stored in the refrigerator is excellent in pastry and bread-making. With last year's goose fat, I made excellent ciabatta-style bread, substituting the fat for olive oil.

Use the goose carcase to make stock, and preserve the wings and drumsticks in a confit for use in the future.

Goose Confit

Confit, whether of duck or goose, is easy to make and well worth doing because you then have a luxurious instant meal on hand. It makes a fine addition to a cassoulet, but it is good on its own, gently reheated in a frying pan to crisp up the skin, and served with potatoes fried in a little of the fat, perhaps some lentils, or red cabbage, or a crisp salad of fennel.

goose wings, thighs and drumsticks
coarse sea salt (25g (1oz) per 450g (1lb) meat)
raw fat from the goose
1 bay leaf
a few black peppercorns

Rub the goose joint all over with salt, cover, and refrigerate for 24 hours. Wipe off the salt, and put the meat, fat and seasoning into a heavy terrine. First melt the fat in the pan on top of the stove and bring it to the boil. Cover, and cook very slowly in a preheated oven at 150°C/300°F/Gas 2 for 2–2½ hours.

When cooked, transfer the pieces to a sterilized preserving jar, boil up the fat, and strain it over the goose. The fat must cover the meat by about 2.5cm (1in) or so to ensure that it is airtight. Even so, I keep it refrigerated until I need it, as I live in a centrally heated flat, not a farmhouse with a larder.

Duck confit is made in the same way. You can also preserve the heart and gizzard in fat, and use them later in a warm salad with potatoes and salad leaves.

Goose Pasties | makes 12–18

This and the following recipe combine to form a homely yet festive dish, which makes marvellous use of leftovers, bits of goose left over from the confit or roast, and the stock made with the carcase. Turkey can produce similarly good leftovers. I like to experiment with sweet and savoury mixtures, something like traditional mince pies, when meat was added to the fruit mixture.

225g (8oz) puff pastry
225g (8oz) cooked goose, diced or shredded
2 tablespoons olive oil
2 tablespoons grated apple
1 tablespoon finely chopped onion
1 tablespoon dark muscovado, or other unrefined sugar
¼ teaspoon ground cardamom
¼ teaspoon ground cinnamon
freshly grated nutmeg
sea salt and freshly ground black pepper
milk, to glaze

Roll out the pastry, and use it to line tartlet tins, also cutting out pastry lids. Mix together the rest of the ingredients, season to taste with nutmeg, salt and pepper, and divide the mixture between the pastry cases. Cover with pastry lids, and brush with milk to glaze. Bake in a preheated oven at 180°C/350°F/ Gas 4, for 15–18 minutes.

Note

Alternatively fill the pastry rounds and shape like Cornish pasties.

Goose and Barley Broth | serves 6–8

1 tablespoon goose fat
1 large onion, peeled and thinly sliced
1 celery stalk, trimmed and thinly sliced
1 carrot, peeled and thinly sliced
1 leek, trimmed and thinly sliced
115g (4oz) shredded white cabbage
85–115g (3–4oz) pearl barley
3 garlic cloves
½ teaspoon dill seeds, or fresh dill
1.7 litres (3 pints) goose stock
150 ml (¼ pint) good dry white wine

Melt the fat in a large saucepan, and stir in the first 4 vegetables. Cook until light brown. Add the cabbage, barley, crushed garlic and dill. Pour in the stock and wine, bring to the boil, and simmer gently for an hour or so, or until the barley is tender.

Roast Loin of Pork, Rum-glazed with Pineapple and Mango Stuffing | serves 4–6

In many parts of the world, pork is the traditional dish to serve at New Year, and here I have given it rich tropical flavours, which harmonize well with the meat. Choose organic or traditionally reared pork if you can.

1 loin of pork weighing 1.6kg (3½lb) bone out
3 sprigs of fresh sage
4 tablespoons rum
4 tablespoons pineapple juice
125ml (4fl oz) stock, water, or wine

For the stuffing
1 small onion, peeled
1 mango, peeled
1 small pineapple, peeled and cored
115g (4oz) soft brown breadcrumbs
55g (2oz) pine kernels
2 garlic cloves, peeled and crushed
sea salt and freshly ground black pepper

Remove any excess fat from the pork, and discard it. Finely chop any meat trimmings, together with the onion and fruit. Mix with the breadcrumbs, pine kernels, garlic, salt and pepper. Make a deep horizontal slit the full length of the loin, and open it out flat. Spread the stuffing over the meat. Roll it up, and tie at intervals, tucking back any stuffing which escapes.

In a heated non-stick frying pan, fry the pork all over until well browned. Place a sprig of sage on a rack, or crumpled kitchen foil in a roasting tin of a size just to hold the meat; place the meat on top, lay 2 sprigs of sage on top of the meat, and cover it with the skin, from which the fat has been trimmed.

Roast in the top half of a preheated oven at 180°C/350°F/ Gas4 for about 2 hours, basting under the skin from time to time with the rum mixed with pineapple juice. The meat juices should run clear when a skewer is inserted into the centre of the joint. If the juices are pink, the meat is not yet cooked.

Remove the pork from the oven, and keep it warm. Skim excess fat from the roasting tin, and then add a little stock, water, or wine to the pan juices. Boil and strain into a jug or gravy-boat.

A gratin of potatoes or a sweet potato purée is very good with this dish; so too are a dish of coconut rice and a dish of black beans.

Medieval-style Christmas Pie | serves 6

The pie, described by an earlier edition of the Oxford Dictionary as 'not known outside England', is still one of the best designed foods for the traveller. Originally, the pie-crust or 'coffyn' was not meant to be eaten, but to hold the filling in place, and keep it moist and fresh in the larder or on its three-day journey in the mail coach. For just as today we send by post clotted cream from Cornwall, puddings from Bakewell, and smoked salmon from Scotland, Londoners, in the eighteenth and nineteenth centuries, could hope to receive from their country cousins all manner of farm produce and homemade baked goods, including mighty meat pies.

This is the perfect dish for Boxing Day, or another festive meal between Christmas and New Year. It uses up slices of leftover turkey, or goose, or whatever meat you chose for Christmas, and trimmings from the loin of pork which I plan for New Year's Eve or New Year's Day.

450g (1lb) puff or shortcrust pastry
450g (1lb) minced pork (use belly pork if you have no pork trimmings)
½ teaspoon each ground cumin, cinnamon, cardamom, allspice and mace
700g (generous 1½lb) turkey in small, thick slices, or collops

55g (2oz) each chopped dates, prunes, dried cranberries and raisins
85g (3oz) chopped almonds or pine kernels
175–225g (6–8oz) chopped, cooked chestnuts (vacuum-packed are fine)
150ml (¼ pint) stock, in which you have dissolved 1 teaspoon or 1 leaf gelatine
2 teaspoons cornflour
beaten free-range eggs and milk, to glaze

Use about half the pastry to line a 22.5cm (9in) pie dish, or spring-form cake tin. Fry the pork in a non-stick pan until it loses its rawness, stirring in half the spice mixture, the rest of which is used to mix with the dried fruit and nuts.

When the meat is cool, put half of it in the bottom of the pie dish, with half the dried fruit and nuts on top. Then add a layer of turkey, the rest of the fruit and nuts, another layer of turkey, and the rest of the pork.

Bring the stock to the boil, and thicken with the cornflour. Pour over the meat, and cover with the pastry lid, well sealed, decorated with pastry trimmings, if you wish, and brush with an egg and milk glaze.

Bake in a preheated oven at 180°C/350°F/Gas4 for 30–40 minutes. Serve hot, warm, or cold, with salads and chutney, or with a green vegetable.

Glazed Chestnuts | serves 8

450g (1lb) chestnuts, peeled
600ml (1 pint) vegetable stock, or fruity white wine
25–55g (1–2oz) butter
25g (1oz) light muscovado sugar

Cook the chestnuts in the stock or wine until tender. Drain them, reserving the cooking liquid for soup or stock for another dish. Add the butter and sugar to the pan, and set it over a low heat until the sugar has dissolved. Shake with the lid on to glaze the chestnuts.

Celeriac, Pumpkin and Walnut Crumble

serves 8

For the vegetables
450g (1lb) celeriac, peeled and trimmed
450g (1lb) pumpkin, raw and peeled
2 onions, peeled and finely chopped
25g (1oz) butter or olive oil
2 tablespoons finely chopped fresh parsley

The crumble
225g (8oz) button mushrooms
150g (5oz) butter
55g (2oz) fresh breadcrumbs
3 tablespoons finely chopped fresh chives
85g (3oz) walnuts, finely chopped

Slice the vegetables to about the thickness of a 20p coin and about 5–7.5cm (2–3in) broad. Blanch the celeriac immediately in lightly acidulated water. Drain. Sweat the onions in the butter or oil until soft, then add the sliced vegetables. Cover with a lid, and let the vegetables 'steam' on top of the onions until tender. Transfer them to a buttered baking dish, sprinkling each layer with parsley.

To make the crumble, wipe and slice the mushrooms, and fry in a little of the butter until soft. This should be done over a high heat to evaporate the liquid. When cooked, chop the mushrooms finely. Mix them with the rest of the ingredients, and spoon over the vegetables. Bake for 10–12 minutes in the top of a hot oven, or finish off under the grill.

For a more elaborate presentation, cut the sliced vegetables into 5cm (2 in) rounds using a pastry-cutter, cook as described above and make into individual portions, a layer of celeriac, one of pumpkin, then repeated, top with the crumble and finish under the grill.

Deep-fried Leeks | serves 4–6

675g (1½lb) fresh leeks
groundnut or sunflower oil for frying

Trim the leeks, and remove the coarse tops and outer skin. Cut into 7.5cm (3 in) lengths, and slice in half lengthways. Shred the leeks into long thin strips. Rinse and dry them thoroughly. Heat the oil in a wok or deep frying pan to a depth of about 7.5cm (3 in) and test the heat by dropping in a cube of bread. If it sizzles, the oil is hot enough. Fry the shredded leeks in batches – shredded so finely, they will cook in about 20 seconds – and drain on paper towels before serving.

Creamed Leeks

Use the same quantity of leeks as in the previous recipe. Trim, slice and wash them thoroughly. Put them into a heavy saucepan with a nut of butter. Cover with a lid, and cook gently until the leeks are tender. Fork to a purée with a little more butter, cream or crème fraiche and a grating of nutmeg. Brussels sprouts can be prepared in the same way.

Gratin of Salsify | serves 4,plus leftovers

1.5kg (generous 3lb) salsify
1 teaspoon lemon juice

For the sauce
25g (1oz) unsalted butter
25g (1oz) plain flour
150ml (¼ pint) salsify cooking liquor
150ml (¼ pint) milk, or 300ml (½ pint) cooking liquid mixed with dried milk
sea salt and freshly ground black pepper
freshly grated nutmeg
55–85g (2–3oz) grated cheese (optional)
25g (1oz) fresh breadcrumbs

Scrub, peel, and cut up each root, dropping the pieces as you work into a saucepan of water, to which you have added the lemon juice. Cut into 2.5cm (1in) lengths, or into 7.5cm–10cm (3–4in) lengths, and then quarter lengthways, depending on whether you want chunky or slender pieces. Rinse and cover with fresh water. Bring to the boil, then simmer until just tender to the knife-point. Drain. You can use some of the cooking liquid for the sauce.

To make the sauce, melt half the butter, stir in the flour, and gradually add the liquid, stirring until you have a smooth paste.

Simmer for 10 minutes, then season and stir in half the cheese, if using.

Combine the cooked salsify and the sauce, and spoon into an ovenproof dish. Scatter the rest of the cheese on top, dot with the remaining butter, and sprinkle on the breadcrumbs. Bake in a preheated oven at 180°C/350°F/Gas4 for 30 minutes, or 200°/400°F/Gas6 for 15 minutes. The leftovers make a very good cream soup.

Stir-fried Kohl Rabi and Chinese Leaves with Toasted Sesame Seeds | serves 4–6

2 kohl rabi
1 head of Chinese cabbage
2 tablespoons sesame seeds
2 tablespoons groundnut oil
2 tablespoons water
2 tablespoons rice, or cider vinegar
1 tablespoon soy sauce
2 teaspoons light muscovado sugar
2–3 teaspoons toasted sesame oil
freshly ground black pepper or Szechuan pepper

Peel and quarter the kohl rabi and cut it into slim wedges. Trim and shred the Chinese cabbage.

In a wok, sauté pan or stir-fry pan, dry-toast the sesame seeds, and put to one side. Heat the oil and in it stir the vegetables until wilted. Add the water and vinegar, put the lid on, and shake the vegetables.

Let steam for a few minutes, then add the rest of the ingredients. Stir to mix well, cook for a few minutes more, and then serve, scattered with the sesame seeds.

Other Vegetable Suggestions

Salsify: cream

Jerusalem artichokes: gratin

Savoy cabbage: shredded and stir-fried with olive oil and sherry or fruit vinegar

Kale or green cabbage shredded and stir-fried with flaked almonds, sultanas and crème fraiche

Sweet potatoes: baked

Pumpkin: baked

Wild rice: cooked in vegetable stock with wild mushrooms

Purées of root vegetables with spices

Chestnuts, small onions and quartered pears: braised and glazed

Puddings and Desserts

Christmas wouldn't be Christmas without mince pies. But there are mince pies and mince pies. Using all the exotic varieties of dried fruit now available, I have developed a richly flavoured tropical mincemeat. I feel sure our mothers and grandmothers would have done the same if they had been able to buy dried mango, banana, pineapple and papaya, not to mention all the fresh tropical fruit so widely available now. To go with the mincemeat, instead of a pastry topping for my mince pies, I make a light crumble topping using butter, flour, light muscovado sugar and desiccated coconut.

A hasty pudding, a marzipan ice-cream, an alabaster pudding and a banana and cardamom fool will all provide easy and unusual companions or alternatives to the traditional Christmas pudding.

Tropical Fruit Mincemeat | makes 2 × 450g (1lb) jars

This mincemeat is suitable for vegetarians.

1 lemon
200g (7oz) dark muscovado sugar
500g (generous 1lb) dried fruit, chosen from the following and chopped small:
mango, papaya, banana, dates, figs, pineapple
225g (8oz) fresh fruit, finely chopped, chosen from the following: pineapple, physalis, guava
115g (4oz) creamed coconut, grated
55g (2oz) chopped blanched almonds
½ teaspoon each ground cardamom, cinnamon, cloves and mace
2–3 tablespoons dark rum (optional)

Scrub the lemon, grate the zest, and squeeze the juice into a bowl. Thoroughly mix in the rest of the ingredients, and leave overnight for the flavours to blend before potting, sealing and labelling.

Mint, Almond and Dried Fruit Pasties | serves 6–8

Here and in the following recipe are a couple of ways of using mincemeat in suitably seasonal puddings.

450g (1lb) shortcrust, flaky or puff pastry
115g (4oz) dried apricots, chopped
115g (4oz) raisins, or 225g (8oz) good-quality mincemeat
55g (2oz) flaked or chopped almonds
25g (1oz) homemade candied peel, or 1 tablespoon marmalade
25–55g (1–2oz) light or dark muscovado sugar
pinch of ground mace
2 tablespoons finely chopped fresh mint
25–55g (1–2oz) unsalted butter, softened
milk, to glaze
a little caster sugar (optional)

Roll out the pastry, and cut out 6–8 circles. Mix the rest of the ingredients, and spoon equal quantities on to one half of each circle, leaving a border. Brush this with milk, and fold over to seal, or make into a Cornish pasty shape with the seal down the middle, and crimp the edges. Prick in one or two places with a fork to let the steam escape. Brush with milk to glaze, and dust with caster sugar, if you like. Bake in the middle of a pre-heated oven at 200°C/400°F/Gas6 for 20–30 minutes.

Note

The last time I made this, I used filo pastry, 3 buttered sheets together for each pasty, and made them into bonbon shapes. If you use mincemeat instead of raisins, use less butter, and if you use mincemeat and marmalade, you can leave out the sugar altogether. The pasties are good hot, warm or cold. Vanilla ice cream goes well with them, as do the usual creams and yoghurts and, of course, custard.

Hasty Christmas Pudding | serves 4

115g (4oz) plain flour
2 free-range eggs
300ml (½ pint) full-cream milk
25g (1oz) caster sugar
55g (2oz) butter
55g (2oz) fresh breadcrumbs
115g (4oz) rich mincemeat

Make a smooth batter of the flour, eggs, milk and sugar. Melt half the butter in a saucepan or frying pan, and fry the breadcrumbs until golden. With the rest of the butter, liberally butter a 20cm (8in) diameter baking dish, and scatter with the breadcrumbs. Using a teaspoon, dot small heaps of mincemeat all over the baking dish, and carefully pour on the batter. Bake towards the top of a preheated oven at 200°C/400°F/Gas6 for 40 minutes.

This is best of all served warm and lightly dusted with icing sugar. Cream, clotted cream, vanilla ice cream, crème fraiche, yoghurt or brandy butter can be served with it.

Banana and Cardamom Fool

This is best made just before serving so that the banana does not have time to darken. To make an unusual fruit fool, for each serving, put 1 ripe banana, the seeds of a couple of cardamom pods, honey or sugar to taste, a little fresh lemon or orange juice in a food processor or blender and process or blend until smooth. Fold in 1 heaped tablespoon Greek yoghurt or crème fraiche for each serving and serve in chilled glasses.

Note

This makes good ice cream.

Christmas Marzipan Ice | serves 4–6

No eggs, raw or otherwise, are used in this expensive-tasting dessert, which can be made from ingredients you are almost certain to have in your cupboard at this time of year. You can dress it up even further by stirring in good-quality chopped, candied peel and fruit, and toasted flaked or chopped almonds.

500ml (18fl oz) water
12 tablespoons skimmed milk powder
200g (7oz) yellow or white marzipan
grating of nutmeg
2 tablespoons amaretto liqueur (optional)

Put half the water into a saucepan, whisk in the skimmed milk powder, and then add the marzipan, in pieces. Set over a low heat, and stir occasionally until the marzipan has melted. Remove from the heat.

Grate on a little nutmeg, stir in the liqueur, if using, and then add the remaining water. Cool the liquid, and then freeze it in a sorbetière, ice cream-maker, or in a plastic box in the ice-making compartment of your freezer. If using the latter method, stir from time to time. Allow the ice to ripen at room temperature before serving it.

Hazelnut Macaroons | makes 24

150g (5oz) ground hazelnuts, plus a handful of flaked nuts
1 free-range egg white
3 tablespoons caster sugar
1 tablespoon cornflour

Mix all the ingredients together, to produce a fairly firm paste. Shape with 2 teaspoons into quenelles (or with coffee spoons to make small macaroons for after-dinner sweetmeats) and place on a baking tray lined with baking parchment. Bake in the centre of a preheated oven at 180°C/350°F/Gas 4 for 15 minutes, then for a further 15 minutes at 150°C/300°F/Gas 2. Cool on a wire rack.

Almond Hearts | makes about 30

150g (5oz) ground almonds
115g (4oz) icing sugar, sifted
orange flower water, to taste
free-range egg white

Mix the almonds and icing sugar, and add a teaspoon or so of orange flower water. Mix in just enough egg white to bind together to a firm paste that can be rolled out. It is easy to overdo the egg white, in which case you will find yourself having to add extra ground almonds. Wrap in clingfilm and chill for an hour.

Roll out to 5mm (¼in) thick, dusting the work top and rolling-pin with cornflour if necessary to prevent the mixture from sticking. Cut out with a heart-shaped cutter and place on a baking sheet, lined with baking parchment or rice paper. Bake in a preheated oven at 170°C/325°F/Gas3 for 15–20 minutes until pale gold. Cook on a wire rack, and sift icing sugar over them before serving.

Golden Fruit Salad

Use some or all of the following fruit in appropriate quantities:

mango
papaya
kumquats
kaki or Sharon fruit
mandarin oranges and other easy-peelers
golden Russet apples
ripe star fruit
pineapple
golden muscat grapes
passion-fruit
physalis
fresh dates
ripe galia or charentais melon
soaked dried apricots
sweet dessert wine, such as Muscat de Rivesaltes or Moscatel de Valencia
2–3 sheets gold leaf (optional)

Prepare the fruit as appropriate, but keep it in distinctive shapes rather than dicing it all: slices of star fruit, long curving slivers of mango, orange segments, melon balls. Leave smaller fruit whole, and be prepared to put up with kumquat pips and grape seeds. Peel any fruit that needs it over a bowl to catch any juice.

Mix the fruit juices with the wine, and crumble in the gold leaf, if using. Put the fruit into a large bowl, preferably glass, and pour the gold-flecked wine over it. Serve chilled. All-red or all-green fruit salad can be made in the same way.

Cider Syllabub | serves 6–8

600ml (1 pint) double cream
4 tablespoons apple juice
200ml (7fl oz) cider
2 tablespoons Somerset cider brandy
caster sugar, to taste
freshly grated nutmeg

Put all the ingredients into a large bowl and whisk until the mixture forms stiff peaks. Spoon into glasses and chill for an hour or two.

Alabaster Pudding | serves 8–10

One of the wonders of the Piemontese kitchen is *panna cotta*, a jellied, moulded cream. Most jelly recipes tell you to use 4 leaves or 4 teaspoons of powdered gelatine for a 600ml (1 pint) of liquid. The cooks I talked to in Asti and Cocconato d'Asti prided themselves on using as little as 1 leaf of gelatine for 6 puddings, each serving 6 people. I have managed so far to use half quantities of gelatine, but it is still somewhat nerve-racking. Will it turn out of the mould, or will it fall out into a heap? I have adapted the recipe to West Country ingredients and now serve it as an alternative, or even as a companion, to the traditional Christmas pudding. I call it Alabaster Pudding.

4–5 leaves of gelatine, or 4 teaspoons powdered gelatine
850ml (1½ pints) double cream
300ml (½ pint) single cream or full-cream milk
1–2 dessertspoons caster sugar

For the decoration
mandarin oranges
pomegranate seeds
candied angelica

Soften the gelatine in a little water, then drain it. Heat both creams, or the cream and milk, to blood heat, then add the sugar and drained gelatine. Stir until both have dissolved, then allow to cool. Before the mixture begins to set, pour it into a wet pudding basin. Refrigerate overnight.

Loosen the jelly by holding a hot cloth to the mould and carefully easing it out on to a shallow dish. Decorate with mandarin segments macerated in orange juice and ruby-red pomegranate seeds, and angelica cut into appropriate decorative shapes.

Spiced Cider Bread | makes a 1kg (2lb) loaf

350g (12oz) plain flour
½ teaspoon each ground allspice, cloves, cardamom, freshly grated nutmeg and ground ginger
pinch of salt
200g (7oz) butter
200g (7oz) light muscovado sugar
2 teaspoons baking powder
2 teaspoons fast-action easy-blend yeast granules
450g (1lb) mixed dried fruit
3 free-range eggs, lightly beaten
about 200ml (7fl oz) dry or medium cider, warm

Sift the flour, spices and salt together into a bowl. Cut in the butter, then rub it in. Add the sugar, baking powder and yeast, then the dried fruit. Mix in the eggs and cider. Spoon into a lined, greased loaf tin, allow to rise and double in volume, then bake in a preheated oven at 150°C/300°F/Gas2 for about 3–4 hours.

Allow to cool in the tin before removing, then wrap and store. Serve sliced and buttered with a mug of mulled cider.

Mulled Cider | makes 1.3 litres (2½ pints)

1.25 litres (2 pints) cider, dry or medium-dry as you prefer
300ml (½ pint) clear apple juice
1 cinnamon stick
1–2 tablespoons light muscovado sugar
freshly grated nutmeg
Somerset cider brandy

Warm the cider in a saucepan with the apple juice, cinnamon, sugar and nutmeg. When the sugar has dissolved, and the cider is very hot, remove from the heat and stir in the cider brandy.

Cranberry, Pear and Walnut Pudding | serves 6–8

225g (8oz) fresh cranberries
2 ripe Conference pears
115g (4oz) walnut halves
85g (3oz) unrefined granulated sugar
3 large free-range eggs
115g (4oz) sifted wholemeal self-raising flour
55g (2oz) unsalted butter, melted

Wash and pick over the cranberries. Drain and pile on a clean tea-towel to dry. Peel, core and slice the pears. Mix them with the cranberries, walnuts and 25g (1oz) of the sugar, and put them into a buttered baking dish, about 5cm (2in) deep, and about 1.2 litres (2 pints) capacity. Beat together the eggs, the rest of the sugar, the flour and butter until smooth, and pour over the fruit. Bake in a preheated oven at 170°C/325°F/Gas 3 for 45–50 minutes until risen and golden. When done, a knife-point inserted into the centre will come out clean.

Christmas Log with Chestnut Cream | serves 6

85g (3oz) almonds
2 whole eggs
2 egg whites
85g (3oz) caster sugar
85g (3oz) self-raising flour, sifted

For the chestnut cream
2 teaspoons powdered gelatine, softened in 2 tablespoons amaretto liqueur, or rum
225g (8oz) sweetened chestnut purée
300ml (½ pint) double cream

Line a Swiss roll tin with baking parchment or silicone paper. Rub the almonds in a cloth to get rid of any dust and loose skin, but do not blanch them. Chop them by hand or in a food processor, taking care not to produce ground almonds, but making sure, nevertheless, that they are well chopped. Put the eggs, egg whites and sugar into a large bowl set over a saucepan of hot water. The bowl should not touch the water. Whisk until pale and frothy and much increased in volume. Remove from the heat, and continue whisking until cool, about 5 minutes over the heat and 5 minutes off is sufficient. Fold in the sifted flour, and then the chopped almonds. Spoon into the prepared Swiss roll tin, and smooth the surface. Bake in the top half of a preheated oven at 200°C/400°F/Gas6 for 12–15 minutes.

Meanwhile, make the chestnut cream. Heat the gelatine gently in the liqueur without boiling, until dissolved. Mix with the chestnut purée. Whip the cream, and fold into the purée.

Remove the cake from the oven, and turn out on to a clean tea-towel, paper side up. Carefully remove the paper, and trim the edges of the sponge which will be crisper than the rest and make rolling difficult. Loosely roll the sponge in the tea-towel. This keeps it pliable. Unroll it, and spread with half the chestnut cream. Roll up tightly, and transfer to a serving plate. Spread the remaining cream over the roll, marking the surface with a fork to represent tree bark and knots.

Quince Purée

makes enough to keep in the refrigerator and to serve with cold meats

2kg (generous 4lb) quinces
1.75 litres (3 pints) water
675g (1½lb) sugar
7.5 (3in) cinnamon stick
115g (4oz) butter
70ml (⅛ pint) cider vinegar

Wipe, peel, quarter and core the quinces. Put the quinces into a saucepan with the water, sugar, cinnamon and half the butter. Bring to the boil, then simmer for 15–20 minutes. Drain, reserving the syrup for other uses such as sorbets. Return the fruit to the pan and continue cooking, with the vinegar added, until tender. Sieve the fruit, and stir in the butter. Serve hot with the main course or cold as a chutney.

Note

Use the quince peel, and core if you like, to make about 300ml (½ pint) pectin-rich extraction which can be used to make jam or jelly with the new season's forced rhubarb.

Cranberry, Kumquat and Juniper Relish

makes about 900g (2lb)

450g (1lb) onions, peeled and chopped
1 tablespoon groundnut oil
25g (1oz) butter
225g (8oz) kumquats
225g (8oz) cranberries
1 teaspoon juniper berries, lightly crushed
1 bay leaf
2 cloves
85g (3oz) light muscovado sugar
2–3 tablespoons sherry vinegar

Cook the onion very gently in the oil and butter until soft and beginning to caramelize slightly. Allow 30–40 minutes for this, and stir from time to time to prevent the onions from burning.

Meanwhile, halve the kumquats, discard the seeds, and chop the fruit roughly. Simmer in 2–3 tablespoons water until the fruit is tender. When the onion is soft, stir in the kumquats and their cooking liquid, the cranberries, juniper berries and bay leaf studded with the cloves. Cover with a lid, and cook over a gentle heat until the cranberries have popped. Remove the lid, raise the heat, and let the cooking liquid evaporate. Stir in the sugar, and add the vinegar. Cook until thick and glossy, remove the bay leaf and cloves, cool, pot and refrigerate.

Index